# ELIZABETH DOLE

WOMEN of ACHIEVEMENT

# ELIZABETH DOLE

Richard Kozar

CHELSEA HOUSE PUBLISHERS
PHILADELPHIA

*Frontis:* Elizabeth Dole has been a groundbreaking woman in Washington, D.C., for over 30 years.

**Chelsea House Publishers**
EDITOR IN CHIEF  Stephen Reginald
PRODUCTION MANAGER  Pamela Loos
DIRECTOR OF PHOTOGRAPHY  Judy L. Hasday
ART DIRECTOR  Sara Davis
MANAGING EDITOR  James D. Gallagher
SENIOR PRODUCTION EDITOR  Lee Anne Gelletly

Staff for **Elizabeth Dole**
SENIOR EDITOR  James D. Gallagher
ASSOCIATE ART DIRECTOR  Takeshi Takahashi
DESIGNER  Emiliano Begnardi
PICTURE RESEARCHER  Sandy Jones
COVER ILLUSTRATION  Cliff Spohn

The Chelsea House World Wide Web address is
http://www.chelseahouse.com

First Printing
1  3  5  7  9  8  6  4  2

**Library of Congress Cataloging-in-Publication Data**

Kozar, Richard.
Elizabeth Dole / by Richard Kozar
p.    cm.    — (Women of achievement)
Includes bibliographical references (p.    ) and index.
Summary: A biography of the woman who has spent much of her life in
public service as a member of the Federal Trade Commission, Secretary of
Transportation, president of the American Red Cross and possible presidential candidate.
ISBN 0-7910-5289-3. — ISBN 0-7910-5290-7 (pbk.)
1. Dole, Elizabeth Hanford—Juvenile literature. 2. Women cabinet officers—United States—Biography—Juvenile literature. 3. Cabinet officers—United States—Biography—Juvenile literature. [1. Dole, Elizabeth Hanford. 2. Cabinet officers. 3. Women biography.] I. Title. II. Series.
E840.8.D63K69  1999
973.92'092—dc21
[B]                                                                    99–15166
                                                                         CIP

# CONTENTS

# WOMEN of ACHIEVEMENT

**Jane Addams**
SOCIAL WORKER

**Madeleine Albright**
STATESWOMAN

**Marian Anderson**
SINGER

**Susan B. Anthony**
WOMAN SUFFRAGIST

**Clara Barton**
AMERICAN RED CROSS FOUNDER

**Margaret Bourke-White**
PHOTOGRAPHER

**Rachel Carson**
BIOLOGIST AND AUTHOR

**Cher**
SINGER AND ACTRESS

**Hillary Rodham Clinton**
FIRST LADY AND ATTORNEY

**Katie Couric**
JOURNALIST

**Diana, Princess of Wales**
HUMANITARIAN

**Emily Dickinson**
POET

**Elizabeth Dole**
POLITICIAN

**Amelia Earhart**
AVIATOR

**Gloria Estefan**
SINGER

**Jodie Foster**
ACTRESS AND DIRECTOR

**Betty Friedan**
FEMINIST

**Althea Gibson**
TENNIS CHAMPION

**Ruth Bader Ginsburg**
SUPREME COURT JUSTICE

**Helen Hayes**
ACTRESS

**Katharine Hepburn**
ACTRESS

**Mahalia Jackson**
GOSPEL SINGER

**Helen Keller**
HUMANITARIAN

**Ann Landers/
Abigail Van Buren**
COLUMNISTS

**Barbara McClintock**
BIOLOGIST

**Margaret Mead**
ANTHROPOLOGIST

**Edna St. Vincent Millay**
POET

**Julia Morgan**
ARCHITECT

**Toni Morrison**
AUTHOR

**Grandma Moses**
PAINTER

**Lucretia Mott**
WOMAN SUFFRAGIST

**Sandra Day O'Connor**
SUPREME COURT JUSTICE

**Rosie O'Donnell**
ENTERTAINER AND COMEDIAN

**Georgia O'Keeffe**
PAINTER

**Eleanor Roosevelt**
DIPLOMAT AND HUMANITARIAN

**Wilma Rudolph**
CHAMPION ATHLETE

**Elizabeth Cady Stanton**
WOMAN SUFFRAGIST

**Harriet Beecher Stowe**
AUTHOR AND ABOLITIONIST

**Barbra Streisand**
ENTERTAINER

**Elizabeth Taylor**
ACTRESS AND ACTIVIST

**Mother Teresa**
HUMANITARIAN AND
RELIGIOUS LEADER

**Barbara Walters**
JOURNALIST

**Edith Wharton**
AUTHOR

**Phyllis Wheatley**
POET

**Oprah Winfrey**
ENTERTAINER

**Babe Didrikson Zaharias**
CHAMPION ATHLETE

# "REMEMBER THE LADIES"

## MATINA S. HORNER

"Remember the Ladies." That is what Abigail Adams wrote to her husband John, then a delegate to the Continental Congress, as the Founding Fathers met in Philadelphia to form a new nation in March of 1776. "Be more generous and favorable to them than your ancestors. Do not put such unlimited power in the hands of the Husbands. If particular care and attention is not paid to the Ladies," Abigail Adams warned, "we are determined to foment a Rebellion, and will not hold ourselves bound by any Laws in which we have no voice, or Representation."

The words of Abigail Adams, one of the earliest American advocates of women's rights, were prophetic. Because when we have not "remembered the ladies," they have, by their words and deeds, reminded us so forcefully of the omission that we cannot fail to remember them. For the history of American women is as interesting and varied as the history of our nation as a whole. American women have played an integral part in founding, settling, and building our country. Some we remember as remarkable women who—against great odds—achieved distinction in the public arena: Anne Hutchinson, who in the 17th century became a charismatic religious leader; Phillis Wheatley, an 18th-century black slave who became a poet; Susan B. Anthony, whose name is synonymous with the 19th-century women's rights movement, and who led the struggle to enfranchise women; and in the 20th century, Amelia Earhart, the first woman to cross the Atlantic Ocean by air.

These extraordinary women certainly merit our admiration, but other women, "common women," many of them all but forgotten, should also be recognized for their contributions to American thought and culture. Women have been community builders; they have founded schools and formed voluntary associations to help those in need; they have assumed the major responsibility for rearing children, passing on from one generation to the next the values that keep a culture alive. These and innumerable other contributions, once ignored, are now being recognized by scholars, students, and the public. It is exciting and gratifying that a part of our history that was hardly acknowledged a few generations ago is now being studied and brought to light.

In recent decades, the field of women's history has grown from obscurity to a politically controversial splinter movement to academic respectability, in many cases mainstreamed into such traditional disciplines as history, economics, and psychology. Scholars of women, both female and male, have organized research centers at such prestigious institutions as Wellesley College, Stanford University, and the University of California. Other notable centers for women's studies are the Center for the American Woman and Politics at the Eagleton Institute of Politics at Rutgers University; the Henry A. Murray Research Center for the Study of Lives, at Radcliffe College; and the Women's Research and Education Institute, the research arm of the Congressional Caucus on Women's Issues. Other scholars and public figures have established archives and libraries, such as the Schlesinger Library on the History of Women in America, at Radcliffe College, and the Sophia Smith Collection, at Smith College, to collect and preserve the written and tangible legacies of women.

From the initial donation of the Women's Rights Collection in 1943, the Schlesinger Library grew to encompass vast collections documenting the manifold accomplishments of American women. Simultaneously, the women's movement in general and the academic discipline of women's studies in particular also began with a narrow definition and gradually expanded their mandate. Early causes, such as woman suffrage and social reform, abolition, and organized labor were joined by newer concerns, such as the history of women in business and the professions and in politics and government; the study of the family; and social issues such as health policy and education.

Women, as historian Arthur M. Schlesinger, jr., once pointed out, "have constituted the most spectacular casualty of traditional history. They have made up at least half the human race, but you could never tell that by looking at the books historians write." The new breed of historians is remedying that omission. They have written books about immigrant women and about working-class women who struggled for survival in cities and about black women who met the challenges of life in rural areas. They are telling the stories of women who, despite the barriers of tradition and economics, became lawyers and doctors and public figures.

The women's studies movement has also led scholars to question traditional interpretations of their respective disciplines. For example, the study of war has traditionally been an exercise in military and political analysis, an examination of strategies planned and executed by men. But scholars of women's history have pointed out that wars have also been periods of tremendous change and even opportunity for women, because the very absence of men on the home front enabled them to expand their educational, economic, and professional activities and to assume leadership in their homes.

The early scholars of women's history showed a unique brand of courage in choosing to investigate new subjects and take new approaches to old ones. Often, like their subjects, they endured criticism and even ostracism by their academic colleagues. But their efforts have unquestionably been worthwhile, because with the publication of each new study and book another piece of the historical patchwork is sewn into place, revealing an increasingly comprehensive picture of the role of women in our rich and varied history.

Such books on groups of women are essential, but books that focus on the lives of individuals are equally indispensable. Biographies can be inspirational, offering their readers the example of people with vision who have looked outside themselves for their goals and have often struggled against great obstacles to achieve them. Marian Anderson, for instance, had to overcome racial bigotry in order to perfect her art and perform as a concert singer. Isadora Duncan defied the rules of classical dance to find true artistic freedom. Jane Addams had to break down society's notions of the proper role for women in order to create new social situations, notably the settlement house. All of these women had to come to terms both with themselves and with the world in which they lived. Only then could they move ahead as pioneers in their chosen callings.

Biography can inspire not only by adulation but also by realism. It helps us to see not only the qualities in others that we hope to emulate, but also, perhaps, the weaknesses that made them "human." By helping us identify with the subject on a more personal level they help us feel that we, too, can achieve such goals. We read about Eleanor Roosevelt, for instance, who occupied a unique and seemingly enviable position as the wife of the president. Yet we can sympathize with her inner dilemma; an inherently shy woman, she had to force herself to live a most public life in order to use her position to benefit others. We may not be able to imagine ourselves having the immense poetic talent of Emily Dickinson, but from her story we can understand the challenges faced by a creative woman who was expected to fulfill many family responsibilities. And though few of us will ever reach the level of athletic accomplishment displayed by Wilma Rudolph or Babe Zaharias, we can still appreciate their spirit, their overwhelming will to excel.

A biography is a multifaceted lens. It is first of all a magnification, the intimate examination of one particular life. But at the same time, it is a wide-angle lens, informing us about the world in which the subject lived. We come away from reading about one life knowing more about the social, political, and economic fabric of the time. It is for this reason, perhaps, that the great New England essayist Ralph Waldo Emerson wrote in 1841, "There is properly no history: only biography." And it is also why biography, and particularly women's biography, will continue to fascinate writers and readers alike.

Scenes like this one at a January 1999 rally in Salisbury, North Carolina, prompted Elizabeth Dole to consider running for president. In March 1999, she formed an exploratory committee to measure whether she could count on similar support from voters all over the country.

# 1

# WHAT IT TAKES

Elizabeth Dole has probably done more to advance the stature of women in public service than anyone in the last three decades of the 20th century. Skeptics may argue that other prominent women such as Hillary Rodham Clinton could vie for this honor because of her activism as first lady as well as her desire to become a U.S. senator in 2000. But Mrs. Dole has accomplished as much as this powerful woman she's frequently compared to—and more.

For starters, in 1999 she set out to do what childhood pals long ago predicted: run for president of the United States. While other women this century have attempted to reach the White House by being elected (including Geraldine Ferraro's vice-presidential run in 1984 and Senator Margaret Chase Smith's presidential bid in 1964), none have been considered serious contenders until Mrs. Dole stepped onto the national political scene as the century drew to a close and announced her intention to become the first female president.

Her ambitious goal came as no surprise to legions of fans who have followed her glowing career, which reads like a grown-up version of *Who's Who in America*, the publication that recognizes noteworthy high school and college students across the country for their achievements. Mrs. Dole had previously worked for three presidential administrations. The first woman to serve in the cabinets of two different presidents, she was Ronald Reagan's secretary of transportation and George Bush's secretary of labor.

Moreover, she served as president of the American Red Cross, one of America's highest-rated charities and yet a business larger than half the companies in the Fortune 500. She was credited with overseeing wholesale change in the nonprofit's blood services program, thereby making the blood it distributes to hospitals safer than ever in history.

Mrs. Dole was also no stranger to the national campaign trail, although never a candidate for office herself. Instead, her political skills were honed in three presidential campaigns she participated in while stumping for her husband, former U.S. senator Robert Dole. During those races, she crisscrossed the country giving countless heartfelt speeches on his behalf, boosting his support while simultaneously having another curious effect: raising her public awareness among Americans. On more than one occasion, voters found her so impressive that several asked why *she* wasn't the one running for president.

Although at the time Mrs. Dole brushed off such questions, preferring instead to enhance her husband's chances of reaching the Oval Office, it's inconceivable that she turned a completely deaf ear to such speculation, especially as the country's attention began to turn to who would lead the nation as a new millennium began in 2001.

When Bob Dole's final presidential run came up short in 1996 against incumbent president Bill Clinton, Elizabeth Dole resumed her post as president of the American Red Cross. Her husband, meanwhile, a perennial power figure in U.S. politics for two decades but now retired from the Senate, retreated from the limelight and eventually became a lobbyist and television spokesperson. But the press continued to believe that at least one Dole still had political ambitions, and Elizabeth coyly did little to dampen those expectations.

Finally, after eight years in her highly visible post as head of the Red Cross, she stepped down in January 1999 to assess her chances of winning a presidential bid. She began by establishing an exploratory committee of trusted advisors to begin testing the political waters and raise campaign funds. Analysts had estimated that to be a bonafide presidential contender, candidates had to raise at least $25 million, an amount initially considered within Elizabeth's reach. And certainly, few political observers thought Governor George W. Bush of Texas, the early front-runner for the Republican Party, would have trouble raising that much money.

The analysts were half right; by mid-1999, the son of former President George Bush had amassed nearly $50 million in campaign contributions, which was all the more remarkable because he hadn't even seemed to try terribly hard to solicit funds. Meanwhile, Elizabeth and several other Republican hopefuls, like former vice president Dan Quayle and Tennessee governor Lamar Alexander, were having more difficulty attracting money from donors, no doubt because many Republicans thought George W. Bush was their best chance to recapture the White House from the Democrats in 2000. And in politics, money always follows the surest bet.

Nevertheless, Elizabeth continued her "unofficial" campaign throughout the summer of 1999, making public appearances and continuing to court donors. She even began discussing campaign issues, something she had religiously avoided doing throughout much of her career in public service. Indeed, that was one of the biggest criticisms journalists had leveled at her over the years: she seemed reluctant to reveal the woman behind her famous, gracious Southern smile.

*One of Elizabeth Dole's groundbreaking jobs in Washington, D.C., was secretary of the Department of Transportation from 1983 to 1987. With her as she is sworn in February 7, 1983, are (from left) President Ronald Reagan, Elizabeth's mother Mary Hanford, Supreme Court justice Sandra Day O'Connor, and Senator Bob Dole. Elizabeth headed the DOT longer than anyone in history.*

Skeptics also pointed out that Mrs. Dole had switched political parties whenever it served her career; she began life as a Democrat, later became an Independent in Washington, D.C., in order to land a seat on the Federal Trade Commission, and finally joined the Republican Party soon after marrying Bob Dole, one-time National Republican Party chairman.

But criticism is to politicians what bad weather is to farmers—it goes with the territory. And at least in early 1999, Mrs. Dole's wholesome image seemed like an appealing option to the scandal-plagued Clinton White House. Who better to follow a man widely accused of sullying the Oval Office than a politically seasoned, deeply religious woman who oversaw one of the nation's most respected charities?

Even national public opinion polls taken in February 1999 showed Mrs. Dole would win a presidential bid if voters had to choose between her and Vice President Al Gore. However, the same survey indicated she would lose to Governor Bush.

But as it turned out, the polls weren't as much of an obstacle to Mrs. Dole's presidential aspirations as her inability to attract significant campaign dollars. By October 1999, she had only managed to raise nearly $10 million, while Bush's tally topped $55 million and independently wealthy publisher Steve Forbes had spent nearly $40 million of his own fortune on his campaign. Meanwhile, Quayle and Alexander had already withdrawn from the Republican race, blaming lack of financial support.

Like Bob Dole had been forced to do more than once in his own presidential quests, Elizabeth saw the writing on the wall. She and her husband came to the same conclusion following an October 17 speech to the National Federation of Republican Women in Seattle.

At a news conference three days later, she said: "I've tried to run a nontraditional campaign rather than a traditional one, bringing countless first-time voters into the political process, as we have sought, together, to make history. But . . . the bottom line remains money."

And with that statement, she pulled the plug on a candidacy that had never even been officially declared. But Elizabeth Dole also held out the prospect that America hadn't heard the last of one of its trailblazing women. "God willing, there are many arenas in which to fight, many ways to contribute," she said. "So while I may not be a candidate for the presidency in 2000, I'm a long way from the twilight."

*Duke University was a jumping-off point for young Elizabeth Hanford. She graduated from the school in 1958 with Phi Beta Kappa honors and a bachelor's degree in political science.*

2

# A SOUTHERN BELLE

U nderstanding Elizabeth Dole requires a journey back in time to her Southern childhood, which began in the idyllic town of Salisbury, North Carolina, on July 29, 1936. For someone who as an adult is seldom at a loss for words, her name was a mouthful: Mary Elizabeth Alexander Hanford. She found the string of syllables so intimidating that, at age two, she announced to family and friends that she preferred the name "Liddy," and it stuck.

The Hanford children were born into a respected Southern family. Despite the miseries that millions of Americans endured during the Great Depression of the 1930s, John Van Hanford, whose family had left Colorado for Salisbury around 1900, managed to eke out a respectable living growing flowers in his greenhouses and selling them to local florists. After the hard times passed, the business he had inherited from his father continued to blossom, and he eventually began importing flowers from overseas and supplying them all over the South. Roses were his specialty.

Mary Cathey Hanford's ancestral roots were sunk even deeper in North Carolina soil, all the way back to the years before the American Revolution. The Catheys were Presbyterians of Scotch-

*One of Elizabeth Hanford's ancestors, Francis Asbury (1745–1816), was the first bishop of the Methodist Episcopal Church to be consecrated in the United States.*

Irish heritage who were among the earliest settlers in North Carolina's Piedmont region, sandwiched between the coastal shore and the Appalachian Mountains. Family history recalls that several Cathey ancestors were signers of documents urging unity among the 13 original American colonies as they struggled to escape the tight grip of mother England.

The Catheys also started the first Presbyterian church in the region of western North Carolina where they settled, calling it Cathey's Meeting House. Another ancestor, Francis Asbury, is credited for co-founding the Methodist Church in this country.

Thus, two centuries later, the family Liddy Hanford was born into was both firmly established and prominent. Her two-story homestead was a brick and stucco Tudor with a graceful spiral staircase, situated in a neighborhood shaded by magnolia trees around similarly comfortable houses and families. "Truth be told, I can't imagine a more loving environment in which to raise a child than the one at 712 South Fulton Street," she observed as an adult.

Her upbringing was every bit the life of a genteel Southern belle, for whom proper manners and appearance are a legacy of pre–Civil War plantation life. But like Scarlett O'Hara in *Gone with the Wind*, Liddy Hanford also knew from a young age what she wanted, according to her doting mother. "She is very willful and insists on having her own way," Mary Hanford wrote in her one-year-old daughter's baby book. Nonetheless, the precocious Liddy soon found out she was expected to get along with others. A year later, after attending Sunday school for the first time, she learned how to share toys thanks to several spankings delivered by her mother.

And after she was caught plastering Valentines on the freshly painted pink and blue walls in her bedroom, Liddy learned not to blame others (especially a much *taller* brother John, as well as a make-believe friend) for her own minor misdeeds. Her white lies led her father to tap her behind the legs with a broomstraw switch in front of her handiwork, which prompted Liddy to burst into tears.

The young Miss Hanford was determined early on to stand out. Encouraged by her brother John, who was himself something of an overachiever, at age three she ran for and was chosen mascot for his high school graduating class. By the third grade, she was elected president of the bird club. She was also a tireless student, excelling in writing, spelling, and especially reading. One summer she whipped through 40 books. The accomplishment spurred her to organize a book club the following school year, at which time she felt entitled to name herself president.

Another personality trait that emerged while Liddy was barely out of diapers was her zeal for doing things perfectly, a characteristic that compelled her to succeed as a youth and teen (but would later haunt her as a single-minded career woman). For instance, as a toddler flower girl, Liddy took great pains to drop petals in carefully spaced distances during weddings, according to biographer Carolyn Mulford, author of *Public Servant*.

Even a note sent home from her sixth-grade teacher highlighted the young girl's eagerness to do everything well: "Elizabeth stood right among the toppers in the achievement test recently, but the thing that gives me the most joy is the quality of her daily work. Nothing is ever too unimportant to do well, which is quite a good character trait to possess, I think. And Elizabeth knows how to take notes, express herself in the written and spoken word, do research work, travel and get the benefits thereof, which are quite accomplishments for a sixth grader. What's more, she is seven months ahead in arithmetic achievement. . . . Such pupils are the reason teaching is always a joy."

Journalists and others have speculated for years just why Elizabeth Dole tries so hard to be perfect, even in her attire, which typically includes meticulously matched dresses, accessories, and three-inch high-heel shoes. She has confessed to wrestling with her tendency as well. Some theorize she was actually an insecure little girl; one teacher went so far as to blame it on her "homely" looks.

A girlhood chum implied as much, recalling that Liddy had naturally curly hair at a time when straight hair was fashionable. And even Mrs. Dole once acknowledged in an interview that she was no beauty as a youngster, describing herself as "skinny, wore glasses from the time I was three. . . . I had braces at one time."

"She was overly conscientious and wanted to please so bad," Liddy's second grade teacher told Mulford. "When Liddy got her [new] glasses, her eyelashes were so long they hit the lenses. That used to worry her. She was a beautiful child."

Another side of Liddy's desire to excel may stem from her eagerness to please her parents, who insisted on setting goals for their children. Her father religiously awakened early each morning to plan his day, a habit Liddy shares. Moreover, she inherited his penchant for being prepared. "Oh man, she was so thorough," her brother told writer Gail Sheehy in a 1996 *Vanity Fair* article. "Thorough in planning, thorough in implementing, thorough in execution, and thorough in wrap-up."

In the same article, Liddy's grade school math teacher, Miss Mary Nicholson, echoed John Hanford's observations, with a spin of her own. "Liddy has never failed to be prepared. . . . It was true then, it's still true now."

But at least as a perfectionist daughter, Liddy didn't disappoint. Mary Hanford has painstakingly documented her famous daughter's achievements in more than 20 scrapbooks from birth to the present. She had put her own dreams of a music career aside—including attending the famed Julliard School in New York—to become a supportive spouse and mother.

"My mother is my best friend," Dole says in *Unlimited Partners*, the autobiography she cowrote with her husband. "She combines traditional graciousness with a genuine interest in everyone who crosses her path. Having abandoned her own career pursuit early on, she poured all the more love and energy into the lives of her children."

The Hanfords' prosperous lifestyle assured Liddy of exposure to all sorts of social activities: piano, tap, and ballet lessons; horseback riding; and debutante balls (where a young woman publicly enters society). But in large part, the Hanford children's active lives were also spurred by their no-nonsense parents, who frowned upon idle hands. For instance, when Liddy had finished her high school homework, her mother would suggest she practice the piano or work on her entry for an essay contest rather than let the remaining hours before bedtime pass uneventfully.

Thanks to her parents' means, Liddy Hanford also explored the scenic wonders of America and Canada on family vacations. These trips, often by train, fanned her passions for seeing the world beyond Salisbury, just as her childhood doll collection sparked the desire. Her dolls included examples from distant countries and cultures, several of which were sent home by brother John as he traveled overseas in the Navy during World War II. This wanderlust for adventures in foreign lands would only become more intense as Elizabeth Dole grew up.

As close as John and Liddy were for children 13 years apart in age, they didn't always see eye to eye. One instance in particular concerned the children's grandmother, affectionately known as Mom Cathey. She lived two doors down from the Hanfords, and was so fond of retelling stories from the Bible to her grandchildren and their friends that she would entice them with lemonade and assorted goodies. In a magazine interview years later, John confessed that he "went around the block to avoid them." Liddy, on the other hand, recalls being mesmerized by the stories, and credits her grandmother's influence for her own deep spirituality today. "My grandmother was an almost perfect role model," she has said.

By the time Liddy was a senior in high school, she had made a profound impression on her peers. One publication had nicknamed her "Likable Liddy." The Boyden High School yearbook surmised—with no explanation—that she was destined to spend her life as "a French interpreter in an airport." And not surprisingly, she was voted the girl "Most Likely to Succeed."

However, a majority of those same 143 classmates weren't yet ready for a girl—namely Liddy—to be school president. Liddy lost the election despite a keen observation made in a speech by her campaign manager: "More and more the modern world is giving women a big part to play. Boyden must keep pace in the world."

While a handful of women were playing a bigger part in the world in the 1950s, Liddy was not yet comfortable charting her own course. Although Salisbury was a two-college town, one exclusively for blacks and the other a religious institution, after graduation she followed her brother's footsteps, attending Duke University in Chapel Hill, a Methodist college originally founded to educate white Christian men. "Quite frankly," recalled Liddy's high school prom date in a magazine interview, "I think Liddy had the same aspirations and abilities as her brother did."

Another of Duke's attractions, however, may have been its separate campuses for men and women. Over 1,000 young women lived and attended classes on the East Campus, while more than twice as many men did the same a mile away at West Campus. Both sexes crossed paths only during classes when a course wasn't

available on their home campus.

Once in school, Liddy decided to major in political science, and broke the news to her surprised mother in the fall of 1954 in her first letter gushing about college life. "I think it would be fascinating to learn about American government, history in the making," she wrote. Her daughter's plans so rattled the traditional Mary Hanford, who had expected Liddy to major in home economics, that she confided with a college professor at the University of North Carolina. His advice: "Let her take political science. We need women in gov-

*Elizabeth (center) stands with her parents, John and Mary Hanford (to Liddy's left), in this 1958 photo that was taken after Elizabeth won Duke University's Algernon Sydney Sullivan Award. Elizabeth has always credited her parents with inspiring her to achieve.*

*As a senior, Liddy Hanford was active both politically and socially. She was elected president of the Woman's Student Government Association, and chosen as May Queen (right).*

LIDDY HANFORD AND ELLEN BRADLEY

ernment. And anyway, they all get married eventually."

What was a proper Southern women's college like in the mid 1950s? Liddy has compared it to a "finishing" school, which emphasizes the social graces and art and literature rather than the physical sciences like math and chemistry. She wasn't far off the mark. Female students at Duke were referred to as "Duchesses," and the freshman handbook spelled out its secret to success: "A Duchess should have the tact and good judgment to know when the occasion requires her to be serious and when to be gay, when to dress up and when to be casual. Everything she does is in good taste and up to the highest standards."

Rules ruled the day: alcohol and jeans were taboo, hats and stockings were the dress code for church, and women had to be in their living quarters by 10:30 each night. Once upon a time, Mrs. Dole recalled years later, dorm room windows had even been painted over so

that young women would refrain from gazing at "passing boys" (and, presumably, the other way around).

Although Liddy had several boyfriends and was immersed in campus life—she was welcomed into an elite, secretive society called the White Duchy—her thoughts were just as often on schoolwork as on socializing. On the eve of a traditional debutante ball in Raleigh, she couldn't help thinking she should be writing a paper examining how the decision was made to use the first atomic bomb.

And one classmate called her "Miss Three-by-Five Index Card" because she often toted a convenient stack of note cards around to scribble down ideas. Liddy fueled her political aspirations by joining or running for nearly every post she could, another advantage of competing on a women's-only campus. In a campaign speech she made while running for president of the Women's Student Government, she mocked former campus restrictions such as screens set up to divide women and men in the same classroom.

Liddy won this presidential race and succeeded, among other things, in having the Saturday night curfew pushed back from 10:30 P.M. to 1 A.M. Sunday. She also drilled herself on the intricacies of *Robert's Rules of Order*, the bible of parliamentary procedure. Why? Because she had been harshly criticized her junior year by the editor of the campus newspaper for conducting disorganized meetings.

After boning up on a copy of *Robert's* all summer, she returned to Duke in the fall, confident she could hold her own "with the legislature at Raleigh."

Now that she was a political science and international affairs major, Liddy's career path was becoming clearer. "Although I didn't have a blueprint of where I wanted to go or what I wanted to do, it was just a natural love of government, of working with people, of selling an idea," she said in Mulford's biography. "I love that part of trying to convince people of an idea. I used to think that I would make a good salesperson because I like to get in there and talk about what I believe in. It was a natural thing to major in political science and run for student offices. That led to Washington eventually."

What's more, Liddy's activities in student government were forging the negotiating skills she would rely on time and again in her career. "She's a good mediator," a friend and fellow classmate also noted. "She doesn't threaten people in the process of trying to negotiate and make things better, which, I think, is probably one of the keys to her success."

One of her favorite mentors from college, and no doubt partly responsible for her growing feminist views, was Woman's College dean R. Florence Brinkley, an independent, inspirational role model who taught English literature. Mrs. Dole later described the teacher she met each Sunday afternoon for tea as "a tall, stately woman who taught students to think for themselves, and to think hard."

Liddy was a willing protégé. Not only did she excel academically, earning Phi Beta Kappa honors, she proved the roles of women were changing—at least in some respects. During her senior year, she was selected the 1958 Leader of the Year for the women's *and* men's campuses, and this time received glowing reviews in the campus newspaper for sparking change at Duke. However, she was also elected May Queen, suggesting that she wasn't about to forsake her femininity for the sake of feminism.

*After graduating from Duke, Elizabeth Hanford was not ready to follow the expected career path of many women of her generation: marry and have children. Instead, she decided to continue her education.*

# 3

# MARCHING TO
# A DIFFERENT DRUMMER

Upon graduation, most of Liddy's female classmates were expecting to marry and settle down rather than pursue careers. But she was now determined to go her own way, despite being assured a job with the family's wholesale flower business—where she could have indulged her passion for travel abroad—and despite going steady with a college beau. "I was pinned to a young man from nearby Davidson College, and though I cared for him very much, I simply was not ready for marriage. Not yet anyway," she said.

Feeling emboldened by her already sparkling résumé, she instead applied for a position at the *Charlotte Observer*, only to discover impressive college credentials don't necessarily guarantee an applicant a job at a newspaper.

Humbled by the experience, Liddy decided to move to Boston, Massachusetts, near some acquaintances. There she landed a job as secretary to the head librarian at Massachusett's Harvard Law School—even though she didn't know shorthand and was a novice typist. Years afterward she observed, "All of us start with something that's not our ideal, but you get your foot in the door and you prove yourself and go on from there into things that will be much more meaningful."

Harvard has always been considered one of the finest universities in the country, and has cultivated some of our nation's greatest minds. A degree from the Ivy League school practically assures graduates of sailing smoothly into professional careers in business, industry, and government. To no one's surprise, Liddy, although a dyed-in-the-wool Southerner, felt right at home.

The Harvard mystique immediately rekindled her love affair with study and travel. Acting on the advice of her mentor, Dean Brinkley, she leaped at the chance the following summer to study at England's Oxford University. English history and government were the proposed curriculum, but Liddy, now 23, left little doubt she intended to sample more than academic appetizers once overseas. She also wanted to feast on the majesty of England's cities and countryside.

Although well endowed in history and culture, England didn't satiate her appetite for exotic places. She decided Russia was an even more fascinating destination, partly because the Communist country was so topical in the news and partly because so few of her comrades had set foot there. She set out to convince her skeptical parents in typical Liddy fashion. Almost lawyerly, she prepared a five-point argument in favor of the adventure, and began ticking them off one by one in a phone call home to Salisbury.

Both parents thought the idea outlandish, largely because the United States and the Communist USSR were bitter cold war foes, wary of each other's motives and policies around the globe. However, Liddy pointed out that Soviet premier Nikita Khrushchev was visiting the States at the time, so it was unlikely a nuclear war would break out in his absence. Before she had finished arguing, her conservative father, who had erected a bomb shelter in Salisbury just in case Russia

ever did launch missiles, relented, saying, "Liddy, if I were in your shoes, I'd do it myself."

Bunny Hanford, the wife of Elizabeth's brother John, observed in *Vanity Fair* that her sister-in-law's strategy had a familiar ring to it. "The way she approached that is really the way the Hanfords approach things, and the way Liddy still does today. Not using her feminine wiles, but being very logical and businesslike and organized. This is her. It's inbred."

On her Russian trip, Liddy Hanford revealed a more daring side of her personality. Rather than stay with a group tour, she struck up a friendship with a young man from Moscow in her group who was returning to

*Moscow was an interesting city for young Liddy Hanford to visit in 1960—the height of the cold war. It took an all-out presentation to convince her parents to allow her to travel to the USSR.*

visit his mother. After Liddy won him over, he agreed to bring his newfound American friend home. But despite her insider's view of life in the Soviet Union, what Liddy remembers most of her visit are not the sights, sounds, and colorful figures, but an uncomfortable ambulance ride to a clinic where she received treatment for a foot infection.

Once back inside the ivy-covered walls of Harvard, Liddy decided to enroll in graduate classes, and she embarked on a dual-degree program combining government study and teaching. In an oft-repeated quote, she said, "The first was my emerging passion, the second a vocational insurance policy. I hedged my bets."

Teaching came naturally to her, and she honed her skills instructing a class of 11th graders in a school outside Boston. To stimulate her students, she pored over volumes in Harvard's library, looking for ways to transform dry events in a history book into compelling, real-life dramas to which her students could relate. Once, she convinced a member of the Boston police force that had gone on strike in 1919 to give firsthand accounts of the labor strife that had brought the city to its knees. Such novel techniques were a hit with students, and Liddy's advisers encouraged her to become a teacher. But instead she gravitated to the strongest pull so far in her life—government.

During her second summer at Harvard, Salisbury's native daughter took the first step on her journey in public service by landing a secretarial position in the Washington, D.C., office of U.S. senator B. Everett Jordan, a Democrat from North Carolina. In his Capitol Hill office, she quietly began seeking out counsel from people she grew to admire, particularly Senator Margaret Chase Smith, a Republican from Maine. Smith's advice at the time was, in the best New England tradition, straightforward: get a law degree.

However intrigued Liddy might have been with the then-novel idea of becoming a female lawyer, she didn't immediately act on any such impulse. Instead, she managed to wangle an invitation to join vice presidential candidate Lyndon B. Johnson's "whistle-stop" campaign by railcar throughout the South. The powerful U.S. senator from Texas was John F. Kennedy's running mate in 1960, and his job was to rally critical support south of the Mason-Dixon line.

Liddy's conservative father, although once a registered Democrat, had joined the Republican party, also known as the GOP (Grand Old Party), when General Dwight D. Eisenhower, a Republican, jumped into the presidential race in 1952. Therefore, John Hanford was hardly enthusiastic that his daughter was collaborating with the enemy.

A friend from Senator Jordan's office who joined Elizabeth on the whistle-stop campaign through the Bible Belt was struck by her political fervor, as well as her interest in young men with bright political prospects. The friend told Mulford, "We kidded [Liddy] and said, 'You are either going to marry somebody going to the White House or you are going to get there yourself.' She was very oriented to politics."

With her horizons expanded even more by the Johnson election-year politicking and by earning a master's degree in education from Harvard, Liddy nonetheless returned to her familiar job in Cambridge, Massachusetts, in September 1960. She would return there off and on over the next two years, as if she still wasn't certain exactly how to channel her political ambitions.

During the next two summers, she worked as a tour guide at the United Nations in New York City. By 1962, however, she apparently had taken Margaret Chase Smith's advice to heart after all, and decided to apply to Harvard Law School. One reason she may have agonized over the decision was that she knew she was once again swimming against the tide of conventional wisdom, for in the 1960s, female law students were looked upon as oddities. What's more,

*Liddy's summer job as a tour guide at the United Nations allowed her to meet people from many different countries and cultures.*

Liddy met resistance from her own family as well as from outsiders.

Her normally supportive brother John expressed reservations, saying, "Here you are, in the golden years of youth. Do you really want to bury yourself in a monastery for three years?"

When she broached the topic with her mother during a sightseeing tour through New Hampshire, Mary Hanford's startled reaction was: "Don't you want to be a wife, and a mother, and a hostess for your husband?" Ever prepared, Liddy had a comeback. "I told [my parents] I wanted to be all those things. In time. But just then I had other aspirations." Even so, the aspiring law student again hedged her bets, also telling her parents that she would decide after her first year whether to continue attending Harvard Law.

Truth be told, Liddy never really intended to quit law school after her first year, which is typically the toughest. Few people could blame her if she had quit, however. By the time she graduated three years later in 1965, she was one of only 24 women in a class of 550, representing a meager 4.5 percent of students. (Today, women make up about 40 percent of Harvard Law graduates.) And the biases that Liddy and other trailblazing women at Harvard faced were far from subtle. In *Unlimited Partners*, she recalls the blunt comment delivered to her by a male classmate on the first day of classes. "Elizabeth, what are you doing here? Don't you realize that there are *men* who would give their right arm to be in this law school, men who would *use* their legal education?"

Even select members of the faculty could be condescending. There was, for example, Professor Walter Barton Leach's "Ladies' Day," when Liddy and the four other women in his 150-member class had to stand in front of the lecture hall and each read aloud a poem they had written. The rest of the time, they were never called upon.

Nevertheless, several of her female classmates went on to prominent careers themselves, including Pat Schroeder, a former Congresswoman from Colorado, and Jane Roth, now a Delaware judge and the wife of a U.S. senator.

But at least initially, the former Duke University May Queen found herself woefully ill-prepared for the cutthroat atmosphere that was the norm at law schools like Harvard. Competition was "fierce," she recalled, something she was not prepared for after four years in a Southern religious university. It wasn't unheard of for students to rip out the pages of a text so fellow classmates wouldn't have an opportunity to read them.

But Liddy, who by now preferred to be known as Elizabeth, once again relied on hard work and determination to make the grade. Her mother remembers her coming home on breaks only to hole up in her room, eating meals there and working for days. Her persistence paid off. By her second year of law school, Elizabeth was elected president of the International Law Club. And before receiving her diploma, she would be named class secretary, a title she would retain the rest of her life.

In the fall of 1965, Elizabeth, now 29, left New England for Washington, D.C., to launch a career in government. After moving to Georgetown, she was hired for a position with the Department of Health, Education, and Welfare. Her long-term assignment was organizing the first national conference on education for the deaf, which meant picking a site, deciding who would lecture, and publishing reports. Two years later, all the planning and preparation paid off when the conference was held in Colorado Springs.

Afterward, Elizabeth returned to Washington with her mission accomplished but also essentially out of a job. In between full-time employment, she decided to visit a D.C. night court, where she figured she could pick up a few pointers on defending people down on their luck. Although Liddy was a lawyer and certified to practice in D.C., she had never gone to court before. An opportunity to use her skills came sooner than she could have imagined. The crusty justice on duty, Judge Edward "Buddy" Beard, spotted her in the audience on her third visit, demanded to know who she was, and then insisted Elizabeth defend a Greek man charged with petting a lion at the National Zoo. The charges alleged that he "annoyed" the caged cat. Reluctantly, Elizabeth went into the court's holding cells to interview her first client, drawing jeers and catcalls from other male prisoners along the way. Although the Greek's command of English was poor, he knew enough to convince Elizabeth he would flee for New York without looking back as soon as he got out of the Washington jail—even if on bond.

Realizing that her only chance at saving the eccentric immigrant from a worse jam was by defending him on the spot, Elizabeth insisted the judge hold the trial that evening. So, with minimal preparation, she went to court. Her opponent, U.S. Attorney Lee Freeman, had been a former classmate and editor of the *Harvard Law Review*. Nonetheless, Elizabeth held her own, especially when she pointed out that the defendant should be able to face his "accuser," even if it was a feline. "I argued that without the lion as a witness, there was no way to know whether he had been 'annoyed or teased,'" she said.

After getting her stubborn client to agree to stay away from the National Zoo, Elizabeth was relieved to

hear the judge rule in her favor. National reporters who just happened to be covering the courtroom that night made sure the oddball case made instant headlines. The only thing the embarrassed prosecutor worried about was that word of his defeat not get back to Harvard Law.

Elizabeth spent the next year representing the poor—and the occasionally colorful—people who routinely are hauled into night court. One client arrested for prostitution turned out to be a man who solicited customers while impersonating a woman.

*Several of the women who graduated in Liddy's Harvard Law School class went on to successful careers. One classmate was Pat Schroeder, who eventually became a member of the House of Representatives. Dole is on the left and Schroeder is on the right in this 1987 photo.*

*Elizabeth Dole had campaigned for Lyndon B. Johnson in 1960, when he was run-
ning with John F. Kennedy. In 1968, she took a job with Johnson's presidential
administration, in the Office of Consumer Affairs. Her first boss, Betty Furness, is
standing behind President Johnson in this photo.*

# 4

# BIRTH OF AN ADVOCATE

I n April 1968 Elizabeth took a position with President Johnson's administration in the White House Office of Consumer Affairs. An acquaintance had alerted her to the open post, but it was left up to her to find funding outside the White House to pay for her job (not an uncommon situation in government). She convinced the head of the Food and Drug Administration to use its budget resources to pay her salary, and she went to work as deputy assistant for legislative affairs under Betty Furness, a former television actress-turned-consumer advocate.

The notion of setting up watchdog agencies to protect consumers was popular across the country, and Elizabeth saw a bright future in the movement. At the time, she was still a member of the Democratic Party, which thanks to President Johnson controlled the Executive Mansion as well as the House and Senate on Capitol Hill. LBJ had assumed the presidency in November 1963 after President John F. Kennedy's assassination in Dallas, Texas. Johnson was easily reelected in 1964, but America's growing involvement in the Vietnam War during the coming years would take its toll on him and the country.

The 1960s were turbulent times, highlighted by extraordinary achievements that were unfortunately offset by civil unrest on a scale unseen since the Civil War. John Glenn was the first American astronaut to orbit the earth; the Beatles took America by storm; and by the decade's end, U.S. astronauts had walked on the moon. Meanwhile, tens of thousands of young Americans lost their lives in Vietnam; the country's college campuses became battlegrounds pitting defiant war protesters against the National Guard; and blacks struggled to gain the racial equality they had long been denied.

Except in the most rural areas of the country, it was hard to avoid the strife of the '60s. But Elizabeth somehow managed to, an amazing feat considering she worked in Washington, D.C., which attracted political dissenters like moths to a flame. After the Reverend Martin Luther King Jr. was gunned down in Memphis, Tennessee, in the spring of 1968, President Johnson had to order the National Guard to patrol the streets of the nation's capital when riots broke out. Many Americans feared that their society was coming apart.

The weary president had already stunned Americans by announcing earlier in 1968 that he would not seek reelection to the Oval Office. His vice president, Hubert Humphrey, proved to be no match for Republican challenger Richard M. Nixon in the November 1968 presidential contest. Nixon, a former vice president himself under Dwight Eisenhower from 1952 to 1960, swept to victory largely because he promised to end the war in Vietnam.

Typically, the election of a new administration brings wholesale change throughout government, where political appointees serve at the pleasure of whichever party controls the White House. Luckily for Elizabeth, her office at least had a future. However, her supervisor, Betty Furness, knew her days were numbered when Nixon won; she left her post in the White House Office of Consumer Affairs. Her replacement was Virginia

Knauer, a Republican and former head of Pennsylvania's consumer protection bureau.

Despite their different political affiliations, Elizabeth quickly impressed Knauer, who observed, "In this very deceptive package is a Harvard-trained brain." Likewise, Elizabeth developed an instant respect for her new boss, who she referred to as "both mentor and surrogate mother." And she soon found herself promoted to deputy of her office, which was renamed the President's Committee on Consumer Interests.

The Committee itself had no authority to act directly on behalf of consumers, who often didn't know where to turn when they discovered they had purchased shoddy merchandise or been the victims of consumer fraud. Instead, Elizabeth and fellow staffers channeled consumer complaints directly to the government agencies with regulatory clout over businesses, such as the Consumer Product Safety Commission and the Federal Trade Commission.

Thanks to the Committee's efforts, consumers today

*The 1960s were filled with social and political turmoil in America. Dr. Martin Luther King Jr. led these protesters across the Edmund Pettus bridge in Selma, Alabama, to protest race discrimination in the South.*

simply have to look at a label to see the ingredients a product contains, whether it is a tube of suntan lotion or a box of cereal. In addition, the agency prodded the government to require businesses to put expiration dates on food and drug products, and to list such vital information as fat content. Americans routinely rely on this information to choose healthier foods.

"What began as just a job soon turned into something of a personal crusade," Elizabeth later recalled. "Underdogs have always appealed to me. As a public-interest lawyer I had already seen how fraud or deception can victimize the elderly and others too young or impoverished to fight back."

But help for consumers might have come much easier had women still not had to prove themselves as worthy as their male peers. Time and again, Virginia and her female staffers faced male chauvinism all too typical of the era. At their first trip to testify on Capitol Hill, with a female lawyer joining them, they were asked by a senator, "Mrs. Knauer, do you have anything against men in your office?"

On another occasion, Elizabeth was set to pinch-hit for Virginia while testifying before the House Appropriations Committee, chaired by Rep. Daniel J. Flood. After Mrs. Knauer stepped out, however, Flood abruptly recessed the proceeding—but not before he muttered over a still-live microphone, "Are we going to let this kid take over the hearing?"

Despite such slights, Elizabeth frequently found herself standing in for her boss, a task that required her to give public speeches. To look at Mrs. Dole today, one could easily imagine that she was a born orator. Even her admittedly biased mother thought as much, telling Mulford, "I think speaking is her talent. She enjoys it. It's never something to worry about. She doesn't seem to get nervous, but she does a lot of scribbling and connecting and changing."

But at least one acquaintance in Elizabeth's past saw

things differently. "She wasn't a totally comfortable speaker," Tim Burr, an intern on the President's Committee on Consumer Affairs from 1970 to 1972, told one interviewer. He attributed her initial unease to the fact that "she always wore very heavy glasses." If glasses were Elizabeth's Achilles' heel, that flaw disappeared when she began wearing contact lenses in her mid-30s.

By 1970 Elizabeth's work on the Committee had attracted considerable attention. She was chosen Washington's Woman of the Year, recognition that undoubtedly established her as a force in the capital. Three years later, another window of opportunity opened when Virginia suggested she apply for a vacant seat on the Federal Trade Commission (FTC). A previous member of her staff, a Republican, had already been appointed to the FTC.

In order to satisfy a law requiring equal representation of political parties among FTC members, Elizabeth changed her voting registration from Democrat to Independent, a political affiliation usually chosen by someone who simply doesn't want to be a Democrat or Republican. People who are registered Independent can vote in general elections, but they are not allowed to help the major political parties select their candidates during primary elections.

Although Elizabeth was well-known in government circles, she quickly discovered that her visibility hardly guaranteed she would breeze right into the empty commissioner's seat. For starters, new commissioners had to be confirmed by the Senate Commerce Committee. Its members weren't eager to rubber stamp another appointee with such close ties to the Republican Nixon administration. Consequently, Elizabeth came up with a game plan, and quietly began courting consumer activists and Washington, D.C., power brokers.

Thanks to the groundwork she laid, she ultimately received Senate approval. However, her swearing-in ceremony was more challenging. Because of an auto accident that required a month's convalescence in traction, Elizabeth had to receive the oath of office from FTC officials surrounding her Georgetown Hospital bed.

The FTC has been an institution for most of the 20th century, originally established as the guardian against abusive practices by giant businesses. In short, its job is to protect the little guy. By the time Elizabeth joined the commission, though, critics claimed the FTC was an old dog with too little bark and no bite. But with a Republican administration in control, change was in the air, and the FTC was granted broader enforcement powers. The commission cracked down on fraudulent merchants and careless nursing home operators, and it launched campaigns to inform single women about their rights to borrow money.

Also during this period, Elizabeth bought a condominium for herself at the Watergate, a desirable apartment complex just a short drive from the White House and Capitol Hill. Ironically, her future husband also had a condo in the building, which was destined to become a household name in 1972 for yet another reason—a botched attempt by Republican operatives to burglarize the Democratic campaign headquarters there. After the intruders were caught by a security guard, newspaper reporters eventually linked the break-in to the Committee to Re-elect the President, an organization with close ties to the Nixon administration. Eventually the Watergate scandal led to the conviction of several top Nixon administration officials for their roles in the burglary and other schemes.

The purge didn't stop there. President Nixon, besieged by Congressional inquiries into his own role in covering up the Watergate burglary and impeding its investigation, decided to resign in August 1974, rather than face the ordeal of impeachment and the possibility of removal from office. Under procedures

*On August 9, 1974, Richard M. Nixon resigned as president of the United States. The scandal that brought Nixon down is known as "Watergate," named for a Washington, D.C., apartment complex where the Democratic Party had its headquarters. A break-in of Democratic headquarters by Nixon operatives, and a subsequent attempt to cover up the White House's role in the burglary, led to Nixon's resignation. The Watergate Hotel was Elizabeth Hanford's home in the early 1970s, and it was also the home of her future husband, Senator Bob Dole.*

laid out in the U.S. Constitution, Vice President Gerald Ford assumed the presidency. He would hold the office for two years, until Nixon's term would have ended in January 1977. The White House and Washington, D.C., would survive the upheaval of Watergate. And Elizabeth's career and life would weather the changes as well. But she had no idea that her career was about to be forever changed by President Ford, as well as by her neighbor in the apartment complex, Robert "Bob" Dole.

*Bob Dole and Elizabeth Hanford announce their engagement, November 1975.*

# 5

# THE POWER COUPLE

Although Elizabeth had met Bob Dole, a senator from Kansas, in 1972 when he was chairman of the Republican Party, their courtship took several months to bud and several years to flower into matrimony. The couple discovered they had many friends in common, and their mutual interests included a love of government service and a passion for privacy. But proving the old adage that opposites attract, they also had pronounced differences.

Elizabeth is an early riser and has an outgoing personality. Bob is considerably less eager to have his feet hit the bedroom floor before dawn, and keeps his emotions under tight wraps. She is uncomfortable unless rigorously prepared to give a speech; he is famous not only for taking a detour from planned remarks, but also for throwing out a written speech altogether if the mood strikes him. And while she is a voracious reader and fact-finder, still addicted to notepads, he has jested that "the only book I want her opening at my funeral is a hymnal."

If Elizabeth has been criticized for going out of her way not to offend anyone, Bob Dole the politician has been accused of the opposite—being a gunslinger who frequently shoots from the hip.

This trait may have come in handy in the daily melee of Congress, where verbal sparring often makes the six o'clock evening news, but his quick, sometimes caustic wit also got him into hot water occasionally. Particularly on the campaign trail, he could be his own worst enemy. During the 1996 presidential race, in a none-too-subtle dig at Hillary Clinton, he made this ill-advised remark about *his* vision of Elizabeth as first lady: "She will not be in charge of health care. . . or in charge of anything else."

That slip of the tongue may have come as a shock to his wife, who had publicly stated earlier that she intended to remain president of the American Red Cross *and* fulfill the duties of first lady if Bob was elected. It also made listeners wonder whether he really believed his wife should be a stay-at-home first lady who contented herself with worthy but benign projects like redecorating the White House and keeping roadsides litter-free.

If Bob Dole at times appeared bitter or sarcastic, there was ample reason in his past to explain why. He came of age in the middle of the Great Depression, the son of a Russell, Kansas, creamery worker whose wife sold sewing machines door-to-door. Midwesterners, like New England Yankees, praise hard work but gave praise stingily. Bob Dole's parents were no different; emotions were something to be kept private, and a handshake was about as warm a greeting as one could expect. Therefore, he comes by his stiff upper lip naturally.

In those dark days in the Midwest, scorching droughts coupled with poor farming practices spawned legendary dust storms that swept across the plains, blowing valuable topsoil away with them. These storms literally blocked out the sun for days at a time, and explain why the Midwestern United States became known as the Dust Bowl during the 1930s. At one point Dole's parents were so hard-pressed to make ends

meet that they moved into their home's basement with all four children and rented the upstairs floors to an oil speculator.

Nonetheless, Dole was determined to attend college and eventually become a medical doctor. Unfortunately, World War II intervened in 1941 during his freshman year, and like thousands of other young American men, the 19-year-old enlisted in the U.S. Army. Two years later, now a second lieutenant, he traveled on a troop ship to Italy and eventually made it to the front lines.

*Bob Dole grew up on a small farm in Russell, Kansas. Both the Great Depression and the dust storms that swept across the Midwest during the 1930s hit the family hard. Young Bob is at left, with siblings Kenny, Norma Jean, and Gloria Dole.*

Just weeks before the end of the war in 1945, while leading a platoon of 50 men on an assault of German positions, Dole was critically wounded, most likely by exploding shrapnel. His spine and right shoulder sustained severe injuries, and one of his lungs was punctured. Worse, he was paralyzed below the neck.

For the next two years Dole practically lived in military hospitals, and he almost died from complications several times. It would take nearly two additional years of recuperation, surgeries, and physical therapy for him to overcome his disabling wounds. And to this day, the most he can grasp with his right hand is a trademark felt-tip pen, while his left hand has only partial feeling.

Once a star athlete in high school and college, Bob Dole's body and confidence were shattered. No one would have blamed him for giving up during those difficult years. However, with the support of family and friends, he vowed to overcome his disability and make something of himself. "Beginning the morning of April 14, 1945, I learned the value of adversity," he wrote in his autobiography. "A handicap can become an asset, I've since discovered, if it increases your sensitivity to others and gives you the resolve to tap whatever inner resources you have."

His resolve was also strengthened by a pretty occupational therapist named Phyllis Holden he met at a Michigan medical center. "Phyllis made me forget my injuries," Dole later said. "She helped me think, not in terms of disability, but of ability. She treated me like everyone else." They were married in June 1948.

Thanks to the G.I. Bill, which paid for servicemen to attend college, in the fall of 1948 Dole started law school. While still a law student, in 1950 he became— at age 27—one of the youngest men ever elected to the Kansas state legislature. He subsequently was elected county attorney, and in 1960 won a seat in the U.S. House of Representatives that he would retain for four terms.

While his years in Congress kept him tuned in to the political comings and goings of Washington, they also insulated him from some of the events shaping the '60s, including the frenzy over a British rock band. Amused by his daughter Robin's fascination with the group, he sent a letter to the British Embassy asking if, as a surprise, the band could schedule a concert at her high school. Unfortunately, embassy officials wrote back, the Beatles would not be able to include Miss Dole's high school on their upcoming American tour.

In 1968, Bob rode the crest of a Republican wave that swept Richard Nixon into the White House, and him into the U.S. Senate. On his first day in office, he penned his first official letter to Robin: "Today is a most important day in my life, and I trust in yours. The days and months ahead will be hectic, exciting ones, but my one hope is that I can share more time with you and your mother."

The freshman senator's note hinted at a fact of life that politicians couldn't escape—their profession placed an unbelievable strain on a marriage. Long hours, trips abroad, and perhaps worst of all, the indignities of being a campaign wife all tested the bonds between a politician and his family. Bob once joked that "anyone who would marry a politician should have his or her head examined." However, he took no solace in that observation during the breakup of his marriage with Phyllis in 1972.

As if his life wasn't in enough disarray, Dole was asked to step down as Republican National Committee chairman in 1973, and barely squeaked out a win in his senate reelection bid a year afterward. The Watergate fiasco had tainted Republicans across the country, especially when Vice President Gerald Ford pardoned Nixon barely a month after he resigned.

The only bright spot during this period for the 52-year-old Dole, outside of being reelected, was marrying Elizabeth, then 39, whom he had been dating steadily for two years. The wedding took place in Washington on December 6, 1975. Their union was toasted by luminaries from President Gerald Ford at the White House to ex-president Richard Nixon in California.

When a concerned friend of Elizabeth's urged her to keep her maiden name after marriage, Bob dismissed the notion on the spot. "I think we want to have the same name. I don't care if it's Bob Hanford or Elizabeth Dole, we want the same name." For some time afterward, Elizabeth did sign her correspondence Elizabeth Hanford Dole, but eventually she dropped her maiden name altogether. She also sold her Watergate condo and moved into Bob's, which remains their home today.

However, their honeymoon was short-lived. At the Republican National Convention held in Kansas City in August 1976, President Gerald Ford was nominated to run for a full term in the White House. The victorious GOP nominee asked Bob Dole to be his vice presidential running mate, because Vice President Nelson A. Rockefeller had decided to step down after the election. Recognizing a golden opportunity when he saw it, Dole accepted. He began planning a strategy to shore up Ford's lukewarm support in the Farm Belt.

Life changed overnight for the Doles. The morning of the call from President Ford, the couple could hear tipped-off reporters jostling outside their hotel room door. Then, word came from Salisbury that the media had already descended on the Hanford household for comment and photo opportunities. And Bob and Elizabeth soon found themselves shadowed by Secret Service protection. Their insightful codenames? Ramrod and Rainbow.

In addition, Elizabeth's future flashed before her eyes: how would her husband's decision affect her career at the FTC? She wasn't even sure she could help him campaign and legally remain a commissioner. However, the law did permit her to take a leave of

*Mr. and Mrs. Dole at their wedding reception on December 6, 1975.*

*Bob and Elizabeth Dole did not have a lot of time to spend on their honeymoon. Just a few months after their wedding, President Gerald Ford asked Bob to serve as his running mate in the 1976 presidential election.*

absence, which she gratefully did. In response to reporters' questions about interrupting her career to campaign, she replied, "I think my own career is a pretty good testament to my belief that women should be able to develop their full potential. Above all, they should be able to choose, whether it's a career, or the role of homemaker and mother, or both. Choice is what it's all about."

Still, no one in the disorganized Ford campaign was exactly sure what her role would be. Some advisers wanted her to play the supportive wife, standing by her husband's side with a permanent smile on her face but scrupulously avoiding any stand on issues. However accommodating Elizabeth could be, she wasn't inclined to play this role. In her autobiography, she says, "[A]s an independent career woman, and an FTC commissioner with ten years of government experience, I wasn't going to spend the whole campaign answering reporters' questions with a demure 'I don't do issues.' I *did* do issues. Six days a week. The genie couldn't be put back into the bottle."

She spent all of one week on the campaign trail in Bob's shadow, and then proposed going on the road alone, speaking to different crowds to cover as much ground as possible. She was a hit, often garnering headlines in local papers the day before her husband showed up in the same town.

Ford showed his commitment to America's farmers by launching his campaign in Bob's hometown of Russell, Kansas. He was the first president since Theodore Roosevelt to set foot in the town in over 70 years. At the ceremony, a tearful Bob Dole told an estimated 10,000 cheering fans how grateful he was for their support. "If I have had any success, it is because of the people here. I can think of all the times the people of Russell helped me when I needed help," he said, then pausing, "That was a long time ago, and I thank you for it." The crowd roared.

As for the rest of the country, however, enthusiasm for the Ford-Dole ticket was more subdued (only half of Americans had ever even heard of Bob Dole the night he was nominated). The team was badly trailing Democratic presidential nominee Jimmy Carter, the governor of Georgia, who set the tone for the November election by promising to remain above the fray. He left the task of political trench warfare up to his aides and to his vice presidential candidate, Walter Mondale, much as Ford decided to do with Dole while he minded the nation's business from the White House.

The senator from Kansas scored some critical blows against the Carter-Mondale team, and succeeded in carrying several Farm Belt states as had been hoped. However, with an economy teetering on recession and Ford still hamstrung by his ties to the fallen Nixon presidency, voters handed Carter a narrow election victory.

Afterward, Bob went back to the Senate and Elizabeth returned to the FTC. But their paths crossed on more than one occasion, and not just on their way to the kitchen. Once, in 1977, they went head-to-head on ABC's *Good Morning America* over the creation of a national consumer protection agency that would merge the operations of 26 separate federal offices into one. Elizabeth and the FTC backed the move, while Senator Dole labeled it "overly intrusive and costly."

During the television interview, he tried to counter his wife's arguments. "If I could just get a word in," he said, only half joking.

"But I'm trying to make my point," Elizabeth politely cut him off.

The interviewer sat back to enjoy the sparring, as did millions of Americans watching at home. Of the letters the Doles received after the show, one suggested to Bob "that if he ever wanted to get anywhere in politics, he had better get his wife to shut her mouth." Another hoped the couple could resolve their "marital difficulties." However, spirited public debates notwithstanding, the Dole marriage was on firm footing.

By 1978, Senator Dole was considering whether to make a presidential challenge of his own. And once again, Elizabeth's role became the subject of debate. Her feminist friends begged her not to step down from the FTC, arguing the move would send the wrong message to professional women everywhere. However, Elizabeth resisted their entreaties and later said the decision she reached was an easy one. In March 1979, she resigned from the FTC to devote her full attention to Bob's campaign.

It was not the first time that Elizabeth, like Hillary Rodham Clinton, put her own career on hold for the sake of her husband's political aspirations—and it wouldn't be the last.

*Seated next to President Ronald Reagan, Elizabeth passes a jar of jellybeans to a group of businessmen. Elizabeth was in charge of the White House Office of Public Liaison, but she would soon be moved up in the Reagan administration to a more important position—head of the Department of Transportation.*

# 6

# THE REAGAN REVOLUTION

Bob Dole was fortunate that Elizabeth stepped down from the FTC; she ended up spending so much time on the campaign trail that people could be forgiven if they thought she was the Dole running for president. She had to shoulder the burden because Senate business frequently demanded his presence. He found himself torn between guiding legislation important to farmers and traveling on whirlwind campaign trips to speak to his Farm Belt constituents in person. All too often, commitments in Washington won out. "Sometimes I think I never really ran for President in 1980," he said in retrospect. "Certainly few people seemed aware of my candidacy at the time."

Making matters worse, his campaign finances were thin and dwindling fast, and so was his initial strength in public opinion polls. After finishing far back in the pack in early primary elections, Bob realized the fruitlessness of staying in the contest and pulled out "at about the time Elizabeth passed me in the polls." Upon reflection, he decided it was simply Ronald Reagan's year to shine and not his.

No longer obliged to campaign for her husband's presidential bid, Elizabeth hit the road on behalf of Reagan, who was the Republican nominee facing incumbent President Jimmy Carter. At some point she had switched party alliances, now becoming a full-fledged Republican. Meanwhile, Bob Dole shored up his own Senate reelection chances to ensure he would have a role working with a Republican administration again. He was right on both counts: Reagan won and so did he. Best of all from his perspective, unexpected Republican upsets in key Senate races gave the party majority control for the first time in 25 years.

Both Bob and Elizabeth benefited from what came to be known as the Reagan Revolution. He became chairman of the powerful Senate Finance Committee, which decided how to spend half the nation's budget, and she took a White House post as head of the Office of Public Liaison. This office had traditionally been used to rally support for previous presidents' policies. For example, during the Nixon years, the department (then called the Office of Public Affairs) could trigger a landslide of mail from its organized support groups nationwide and direct it to members of Congress to sway their opinions.

Under Reagan's reign, the office not only succeeded in winning economic reform battles in Congress by marshaling support among business, industry, and the public, it acted as a kind of public relations firm that sampled public opinion and also tried to dampen opposition to White House initiatives. The outpouring of support the office sparked on behalf of Reagan tax cuts in 1981 overwhelmed Democratic phone switchboards and Congressional resistance, leading Democratic House Speaker Tip O'Neill to call it "a telephone blitz like this nation has never seen."

Although Elizabeth continued to excel in her White House position, she had reached a point in her career where she questioned whether all her accomplishments, power, and prestige were worth the emotional cost of achieving them. In fact, despite her outward successes, she felt spiritually drained inside. She blamed her discontent on her driving career. "More specifically, the Holy Grail of public service became very nearly all-consuming," she said later. "I was satisfied with nothing less than my best. Understandable enough but, as you can imagine, it becomes pretty demanding when you're trying to foresee every difficulty and realize every opportunity.

"Gradually," she added, "over a period of years, I realized that though I was blessed with a beautiful marriage and a challenging career, my life was close to spiritual starvation."

The emptiness Elizabeth felt led her to join a Methodist church group of fellow Washingtonians seeking a balance between spirituality and their everyday stressful lives. At these weekly meetings she was forced to confront the source of her own inner conflict: "I came face to face with a compulsion to do things right, and the companion drive to constantly please," she confessed in her autobiography.

Bob Dole once suggested the roots of his wife's dilemma. "Elizabeth comes from a family of perfectionists, so she has a natural tendency to dwell on what she sees as her own imperfections," he said. "Over the years, I've tried to convince her that life is too short to worry about yesterday, and perfection is an impossible standard."

Elizabeth credits her sessions with the church group for convincing her that she can take time from her hectic schedule to stop and smell the roses, whether that means attending church each Sunday with Bob, staying in close touch with friends, or reading the Bible 30 minutes each day. Moreover, the handful of church members she confided in about spiritual matters also counseled her on professional affairs. They, and not political advisers, helped her decide to take the next big step forward in her career.

*As secretary of transportation, Elizabeth Dole promoted automobile safety. In one publicized stunt she and a crash-test dummy greeted DOT employees as they pulled into the office parking lot, cheering those who were wearing seat belts. During her tenure, she pushed for mandatory seat belt and air bag regulations for automakers, as well as another car safety feature, a third brake light that was often called the Liddy light.*

In early 1983, President Reagan offered Elizabeth a post in his cabinet, a group of his most important advisors. The members of the cabinet oversee different branches of government, such as defense, transportation, agriculture, health, and foreign affairs. Being a cabinet-level secretary is a plum assignment, one which Elizabeth couldn't pass up. She would run the Department of Transportation (DOT), which had over 100,000 employees nationwide and a $27 billion budget.

And although there were the usual political misgivings about whether she and Bob would work too closely on the same projects—and therefore create a conflict of interest—Elizabeth easily won Senate confirmation in February 1983. Her chances were boosted considerably when she was introduced to members of the Commerce Committee by Senator Dole himself, who quipped, "I only regret that I have but one wife to give for my country's infrastructure."

Being confirmed as secretary of transportation was the easy part. Overseeing its many functions was a tougher nut to crack. Although few people know it, the DOT's mission statement is vast. It is responsible for writing regulations governing auto, airline, maritime, and railroad safety, as well as disbursing funds for transportation that Congress has approved for highway and bridge projects throughout the country. The Department of Transportation also fights the war on drugs through the Coast Guard, a service branch under its jurisdiction.

Elizabeth was the first woman ever appointed to the position, but her first week on the job gave her little time to celebrate. The nation's independent truck drivers went on strike in protest over taxes levied against them. After the walkout was settled by boosting the diesel fuel tax instead, she was warned by Washington insiders to avoid public safety issues at all costs if she wanted to stay out of trouble. Ironically, however, that was the one area in which she made her biggest strides at DOT.

Her first campaign was to add a third brake light in the rear window of new automobiles. Studies had predicted that the relatively inexpensive feature—about $20 per car—would prevent close to one million rear-end car crashes a year. Thanks to Elizabeth's efforts, the new fixtures, which came to be called "Liddy lights," became standard equipment on new cars.

The DOT secretary's next public safety mission, in 1984, took more finesse. Legislation requiring air bags for autos had a long history of being proposed, opposed, and disposed of during previous administrations. Elizabeth was determined to resurrect the issue, firmly convinced that far too many lives were being needlessly lost in accidents on U.S. highways. Her task was complicated by the expense of air bags (estimated at $800 apiece), resistance from major auto manufacturers, and political infighting.

The plan she settled on was cleverly crafted. Mrs. Dole ordered that new cars—starting gradually in 1986 but rising to 100 percent by 1989—must contain either front-seat air bags or automatic seat belts. However, if states representing two-thirds of the nation's population voted for mandatory seat-belt laws by 1989, the air-bag regulation wouldn't go into effect.

Car companies couldn't complain because they strongly preferred seat-belt laws to the pricey air-bag option, and this was their chance to lobby for the legislation. In addition, seat belts were already mandatory in new cars. The Reagan White House, on the other hand, although typically against additional government regulation, agreed not to disagree with the proposal.

At Mrs. Dole's request, air bags were installed in 500 government vehicles to test their safety and reliability. Meanwhile, states began enacting mandatory seat-belt laws as hoped, starting with New York. Mario Cuomo, the Empire State's governor, had no qualms about backing the legislation; he credited his seat belt for sparing him from serious injury in a car crash the day before he signed the law.

Today, 49 states require drivers to buckle up, and yet all 1999 model cars are also equipped with driver and front-passenger air bags. It's estimated that over 65,000 lives were saved from 1982 to 1994 thanks to seat belts, and over one million injuries prevented.

Another safety issue championed by the Dole DOT was a crackdown on drunk driving and drug abuse. Because of her efforts, every state in the country has now raised the minimum age at which adults can drink from 18 to 21. In addition, she implemented mandatory random-drug testing of the employees in every transportation industry overseen by her department,

including railroad workers, air traffic controllers, truck drivers, and pilots. The practice drew immediate criticism, mostly from union leaders, but it has also proven time and again that drug and alcohol use has been a contributing factor in assorted accidents and crashes involving the public.

But for all her successes at DOT, Mrs. Dole nonetheless took heat for not making progress on other issues, such as strengthening the nation's air traffic control system. Seven months after Reagan took office in 1981, his first DOT secretary, Drew Lewis, fired 11,500 unionized air traffic controllers nationwide for walking out on what the administration claimed was an illegal strike. Management personnel filled in temporarily for the ousted controllers to guide the country's airliners,

*President Reagan and Elizabeth Dole hold up a mock check for $1.575 billion— the proceeds from the sale of the government's stock in Conrail. The process of dumping the federally held railroad was a long and difficult one for Dole.*

and replacement workers were hurriedly trained and put on the job, but several years later there still weren't as many controllers as before the strike. Near-misses in the skies led many people to question just how safe flying was.

Then there was uproar over Mrs. Dole's handling of the government's sale of Consolidated Rail Corporation (Conrail), the Northeast railroad system the government had taken over to save from financial collapse but now wanted to unload. Two of Ronald Reagan's biggest goals as president were to shrink the size of government and reduce regulations on business, so selling a federally run railroad seemed like the perfect plot for the former Hollywood movie star. Unfortunately, politicians and businessmen don't always follow the script suggested to them.

In 1976, the federal government had taken over six bankrupt railroads: Penn Central, Reading, Central Railroad of New Jersey, Erie Lackawanna, Lehigh and Hudson River, and Lehigh Valley. The railroads were combined into one entity, duplicate lines were eliminated, and operating costs were slashed. By June 1981, Conrail had posted its first profit. The government had not intended to stay in the railroad business once Conrail was financially secure, so it made plans to return the corporation to the private sector over the next few years.

Through a competitive bidding process, the railroad company Norfolk Southern had submitted the highest offer, $1.2 billion, to take over Conrail. Nonetheless, many people thought the price too low, partly because the government had dumped $7 billion into the railroad to keep it afloat and partly because Conrail had $800 million in cash and had earned a $500 million profit in 1984. In addition, many feared a sale to Norfolk Southern would reduce competition and raise shipping costs.

Although Elizabeth Dole supported the sale to Norfolk Southern, some Democratic and Republican legislators had their own ideas, including selling the railroad system publicly by offering shares of stock in Conrail for investors to buy. In 1986, the Senate approved Mrs. Dole's plan to sell the line to Norfolk Southern. But the House of Representatives refused to sanction the sale. Instead, it pushed for the public stock offering. Eventually, Reagan agreed to sign a bill that put Conrail stock up for public sale.

In the end, few could imagine how long it would take the government to shed itself of Conrail. Unloading the railroad had first been proposed in 1981; however, the deal wasn't officially consummated until March 1987, when shares of the company were sold for nearly $1.6 billion, at that time the largest public stock offering in U.S. history. The sale had been one of Elizabeth's toughest challenges in her career, and didn't end exactly as she'd hoped. Moreover, despite the Reagan administration's philosophy of selling off government-run businesses to the private sector, the tortured history of the Conrail deal actually made it less likely other government entities would go up for sale.

*In 1988, Elizabeth Dole was named to her second cabinet post. This time, she would run the Department of Labor under President George Bush.*

# 7

# LABORING MIGHTILY

By 1987, Elizabeth's career was once again being influenced by her husband's political ambitions. One of the most powerful members of the Senate, Bob had announced that he would run for president in 1988. He was anxious to continue the Republican imprint left on the country by Ronald Reagan, who was halfway through his second and final term. "I felt that I could protect what President Reagan had begun against the furious counterassault sure to be launched by Democrats on Capitol Hill and special interests whose professed love of democracy never quite extended to accepting the legitimacy of Ronald Reagan's two land-slide victories," he wrote years later.

Elizabeth was faced with a no-win proposition: she could finish out her cabinet position until Ronald Reagan's term ended in 1988, having already served longer than any previous transportation secretary, or she could step down and improve her husband's odds of winning the nomination. This time, there would be no leave of absence. Her decision to leave DOT to campaign for Bob was, once again, widely questioned by feminists and even some members of her staff, who noticed that their boss was uncharacteristically

*Elizabeth bangs a large gavel to start the 1988 Republican National Convention. Although her husband's second presidential bid was a failure, GOP candidate George Bush considered both of the Doles as possible running mates. That job eventually fell to a young senator from Indiana, Dan Quayle.*

troubled over the latest developments.

But at least publicly Elizabeth downplayed the drama, saying in her autobiography, "The decision was mine and mine alone, and I made the decision that was right for me—just as I would in 1995. Not because I had to, but because I wanted to. And isn't that what we women have fought for all these years—the right to make our own decisions about our careers and our families?"

Competition among Republican contestants was fierce, starting with Vice President George Bush, who after eight years in the Reagan White House was considered the logical heir to Reagan's throne. But the Dole campaign surprised nearly everyone with a decisive primary victory in Iowa, a Farm Belt state like his native Kansas. Surprisingly, Bush finished third in the polling behind television evangelist Pat Robertson.

However, the tables turned in the vice president's favor in the next important primary battle in New Hampshire. Bush, a Texas resident who had grown up in New England, soundly defeated Dole. And although the senator's wounded campaign managed a few more primary victories in the weeks ahead, by March 1988 Dole realized the futility of remaining in the race and announced he was throwing in the towel. He would later joke that the night he withdrew from the primary, he slept like a baby: "Every two hours I woke up and cried."

The only campaigning he or his wife would do the remainder of the year would be on behalf of Bush, who went on to handily beat Democratic challenger Michael Dukakis of Massachusetts for the presidency. In gratitude for their loyalty, Bush put both Elizabeth and Bob on the "short list" of vice presidential candidates he was considering. But the job instead went to J. Danforth Quayle, a senator from Indiana most remembered for criticizing the single-parent lifestyle of the television character Murphy Brown and his periodic verbal bloopers, like insisting to an elementary school class that the word *potato* really ended with an *e*.

Elizabeth found herself contemplating what step to take next on her career ladder, and she signed on with an agency that booked speaking engagements for its clients. Because of her glowing reputation, she received thousands of invitations a year to speak, and the engagements would earn her a tremendous amount of money. But Elizabeth was Christmas shopping in Salisbury when another opportunity presented itself. President-elect Bush phoned to offer her a cabinet-level post, this time as secretary of the Department of Labor (DOL). It's hard to say whether he wanted Mrs. Dole because of her public service experience, in gratitude for her and Bob's campaign support, or because she was a woman. Perhaps it was a combination of all three.

In any event, after considering the offer for several

days, Elizabeth, by now a seasoned Washington insider, decided to join Bush's team. She told her hometown paper, "I think the key to a cabinet position is understanding Washington, knowing how the cabinet works, understanding the relationships and how to move the president's agenda forward—and knowing the players."

And as he had in 1983, Republican leader Bob Dole again introduced his wife at her Senate confirmation hearing. After noticing all the television cameras broadcasting the event, he wisecracked: "If I'd had this much coverage in the primaries, I'd be working on my inaugural address."

Although her confirmation vote was unanimous, some Democratic senators seized the occasion to urge her to support a medical leave act, whereby new parents could take unpaid time off from their jobs following the birth of a child. During the hearing, Mrs. Dole vowed to oppose such a plan if it would "slow economic growth and limit the opportunity for jobs."

Elizabeth Dole was only the second woman ever appointed secretary of labor. She took the reins of a department that had been defining and defending the rights of American workers for 75 years.

One of her first goals was to bolster existing job-training programs for men and women to prepare them for the shifting sands the American workplace had become. Across the country, companies were "downsizing"—laying off thousands of employees, many of whom had expected to work in the same job for a lifetime. Instead, they now found themselves looking for new jobs for which their old skills were a poor match. Moreover, U.S. employers had been complaining in recent years that the educational skills of new job applicants were slipping at the same time global competition was pressuring American industry to make better products at lower costs.

Mrs. Dole also began steadily advancing the causes of women and minorities in the workplace. DOL surveys indicated that fewer than 10 percent of the managerial positions in a study group of companies were held by women or minorities. One of the specific problems she examined was the real effect of the "glass ceiling," a term coined to describe the invisible barriers women ran into as they tried to climb the corporate ladder in a business world dominated by men.

In *Public Servant*, Elizabeth is quoted as telling a women's group in England that "there can be little doubt that a woman, no matter how well schooled, what her age, or how thick her portfolio of credentials, enters many business organizations with limited or no hope of reaching the top. The positions of power and decision-making in business are still held primarily by men." She also notes that only two of the nation's 500 largest companies have women as chief executive officers.

On her own Department of Labor staff, meanwhile, half of the employees were women or minorities. Even Senator Dole had done his part to promote women's equality, by naming the first female chief of staff and secretary of the Senate in the upper chamber's history.

One of Mrs. Dole's most formidable challenges at DOL, however, was dealing with the bitter labor dispute over pension health benefits between 1,700 members of the United Mine Workers (UMW) and the Pittston Coal Company. She had monitored the six-month-old strike and communicated separately with both sides. But in October 1989, fearing an outbreak of violence as the stalemate continued, she visited a Virginia mining town to see firsthand the toll the strike was taking.

A day later, she invited UMW president Richard L. Trumka and Pittston chairman Paul Douglas to meet face-to-face in her Washington office. Until then, talks between the two sides had consisted of proposals being shuttled back and forth from negotiators camped out in separate rooms. Justifying her intervention, Mrs. Dole

*One of Elizabeth's biggest victories as secretary of labor was the successful resolution of the Pittston Coal-United Mine Workers labor dispute in 1989. Negotiations in the lengthy strike had been acrimonious until Elizabeth became involved. She opened a dialogue with Pittston chairman Paul Douglas (left) and UMW president Richard Trumka.*

said, "I feel frustration with the impasse. We're talking about communities being torn apart, and in some cases families torn apart as I've heard talking with miners."

However, she also took pains not to raise hopes of a settlement. "I'm not a mediator. I'm not here to say I have the answer to this complex problem. But I do feel now it is time to see if we can facilitate the bargaining process."

Her strategy was to bring the warring chieftains to the peace table by breaking bread with them. She ushered Trumka and Douglas into her office for a private pow-wow while attorneys for both factions remained outside. Then, over coffee and a prearranged lunch, she helped thaw the icy atmosphere between the two men, who both conceded they were looking for a resolution.

Mrs. Dole suggested bringing in a "supermediator," someone who was skilled in resolving labor conflicts and yet acceptable to both sides. That choice ended up being Bill Usery, a former labor secretary himself. Usery oversaw weeks of intensive negotiations between the miners and Pittston. Finally, a settlement was struck on December 31, 1989.

As secretary of labor, Elizabeth had other occasions to celebrate as well, including winning budgetary battles within the administration. In 1990, for example, she convinced President Bush to propose boosting the Occupational Safety and Health Administration (OSHA) budget by nearly $21 million. Previously, the Reagan administration had limited budget supplements because the agency was hardly a favorite of business-friendly conservatives. But Dole appealed for the extra funds to hire additional workplace safety inspectors and therefore crack down on hazardous working conditions.

One of her first targets was businesses that ignored child-labor laws, which had been adopted in the late 1800s to prevent children from working in inhumane or unsafe conditions. A century later, however, minors were no longer making headlines for losing limbs or their lives in factories. In fact, due to growing labor shortages, most underage workers were likely to be flipping hamburgers in fast-food restaurants.

Nevertheless, during one week in March 1990, over 500 U.S. Labor Department inspectors conducted 3,000 surprise raids around the country in a sting called Operation Child Watch. The DOL inspectors said almost half the businesses they searched had violations. But oddly enough, the 14- to 16-year-old juveniles they discovered working were not exactly begging to be saved. In fact, they said the reason they were working long hours after school was to earn money to buy autos and clothes.

Despite the students' protests, Mrs. Dole promised to continue the crackdown, agreeing with certain other critics that teens needed to spend more time improving their education and less on padding their wallets.

*As president of the American Red Cross, Elizabeth Dole oversaw the enormous agency's project to overhaul its procedures for collecting blood. The project, called "transformation," took years and cost $287 million to implement.*

# 8

# MISSION POSSIBLE

After 18 months heading DOL, Elizabeth was quietly courted by another organization that sorely wanted her to take over its management. And for once, the job wasn't centered around government. Still, the task would involve running what amounted to a $2 billion business, one with over 30,000 employees, a million volunteers, and ties across the globe.

The entity inviting her to be its president was the American Red Cross, an enormous, revered charity whose mission includes collecting, testing, and distributing blood; teaching lifesaving classes; coordinating disaster-relief operations; and arranging communications between civilians and armed services personnel overseas.

Red Cross officials had asked Mrs. Dole to consider the presidency shortly after she became secretary of labor, but because she was so new to the cabinet job, she declined to consider the offer. By the summer of 1990, however, with an established track record at DOL, she was once again approached. The Red Cross hierarchy still hadn't found a suitable candidate to lead the world's largest humanitarian organization, which had been founded over a century earlier by Clara Barton. Would she consider the job again?

This time, Elizabeth said yes.

There were rumors that she left the Department of Labor because she hadn't enjoyed her job, that she had no real clout within the Bush administration, and that she was weary of watching her husband waging budget battles with the White House. But Mrs. Dole saw the move as coming full circle to the missionary work that had always inspired her. A childhood girlfriend of Elizabeth told the *Salisbury Post:* "I really don't think she's as interested in her career as she is in making a difference in lives. I think for her that it's almost like fulfilling a calling, that she can make a difference in the lives of other people and in the world, rather than in any political gains that she might make."

Elizabeth packed up and left the DOL in December 1990, and spent her first day at the Red Cross Washington headquarters on February 1, 1991. One of her first acts as president was to announce that she would not accept the $200,000 salary due her first year. "What better way was there, I had concluded, to let the army of one-and-a-half million volunteers know that they are the heart and soul of the Red Cross?" she wrote in *Unlimited Partners.*

At the time, the Red Cross was poised to play a vital role in a tense military mission in the Mid-East—the Persian Gulf War. With George Bush as commander in chief, America had launched air strikes and ground assaults to drive invading Iraqis out of Kuwait, a tiny but oil-rich U.S. ally. Before the bombs and bullets had even begun flying, many U.S. officials feared massive American casualties, some of which might result from use of the biological weapons that Iraq was known to have stockpiled.

As a result, the Red Cross had geared up its blood collection operations to begin shipping as much as 7,000 units of blood a day to U.S. forces in the Gulf. More than 150 disaster workers and medical personnel had already flown to Saudi Arabia to set up the vital

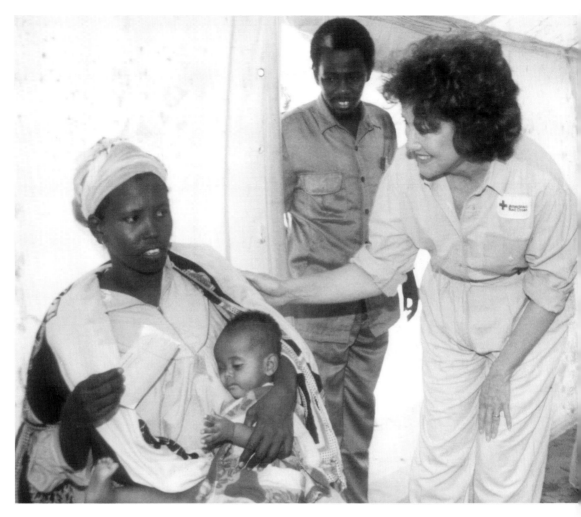

communications link the Red Cross historically pro-
vided between U.S. troops and their stateside families.

As it blessedly turned out, far fewer American
soldiers (less than 300) were killed or wounded than
had been predicted. In fact, the Iraqi military suffered
extraordinary casualties by comparison. But the
Kuwaiti civilian population had also suffered at the
hands of the invading army, a fact that Mrs. Dole
quickly learned on her first trip to Kuwait following the
war's conclusion. She toured a hospital filled with
Kuwaiti children with physical and mental disabilities.

*When the Red Cross tried
to help people in foreign
countries, Elizabeth Dole
was always there. Following
the 1991 Gulf War, she
promised assistance to
Kuwaiti families whose lives
had been devastated by the
fighting. Here, she visits
a Somali woman in
violence-torn Mogadishu
during 1992.*

Over a hundred had died during the war, and the remaining 300 were in desperate need of medical attention. On the spot, Mrs. Dole promised to send 50 doctors, nurses, and medical personnel to help the poorly staffed hospital care for the children, even though her Red Cross staffers warned that such matters usually fell under the jurisdiction of the International Red Cross.

As she returned to the United States, only a month after taking over the Red Cross, Mrs. Dole realized that her new job was filling her with a missionary zeal she had never before experienced. Her own mother had felt similarly moved as a Red Cross volunteer during World War II. "Elizabeth," Mary Cathey Hanford had told her daughter, "nothing I ever did made me feel so important."

Mrs. Dole would need all the inspiration she could muster for the formidable challenges that awaited her back at Red Cross headquarters in Washington. In early 1991, on the eve of the the Red Cross's 50th anniversary of supplying blood to American hospitals, the agency that collected nearly half the nation's blood had come under fire from regulatory agencies and Congress over safety concerns.

For decades, the Red Cross screened blood drawn from volunteer donors for only two diseases. By 1991, however, deadly infectious diseases like hepatitis and HIV and AIDS were threatening the safety of the nation's blood supply. Now, eight separate tests had to be performed to ensure the safety of blood collected. Otherwise, contaminated blood products could pass on these hideous diseases to unsuspecting recipients. Hemophiliacs, who require regular transfusions because they bleed so easily, were especially vulnerable.

The Red Cross blood collection program Mrs. Dole inherited was hard-pressed to meet the demands and extraordinary safeguards now required to handle blood safely. It had 54 testing labs all over the country, each operating independently of the others. Several were cited by the U.S. Food and Drug Administration (FDA) for not following testing procedures or for keeping inaccurate records. The FDA had been hounding the Red Cross since 1988 to clean up its act, accusing national headquarters of failing to track donors and adequately test blood for disease.

To deal with the crisis, Mrs. Dole proposed a massive overhaul of the blood program. Her radical plan was known as "transformation." It would take years, and millions of dollars, to complete. The outdated blood centers were replaced by nine new, state-of-the-art facilities strategically located across the country. Each was linked by a sophisticated central computer system and governed by standard operating procedures to guarantee quality control. To teach staffers the latest techniques in handling and documenting donated blood, a new training center was also constructed.

As in previous posts, Mrs. Dole relied on reams of research and advice from Red Cross staffers before implementing transformation. At one point, she reportedly even considered making blood services a separate, independent unit. Instead, she settled on the sweeping reorganization plan that would essentially take blood services oversight out of the regional branches and place it under centralized control.

Years later, Red Cross insiders credited her for instituting change at a time when it was drastically needed. "She was consistently, forcefully behind what the staff thought needed to be done to fix things," Jeffrey McCullough, former vice president in charge of Red Cross Blood Activities, told the *Wall Street Journal* in 1999.

Transformation has even earned praise from the Clinton White House. Secretary of Health and Human Services Donna Shalala, testifying before Congress in 1996, said she "can't say enough good about what the Red Cross has done. They have made a huge investment in improving the quality of their own oversight

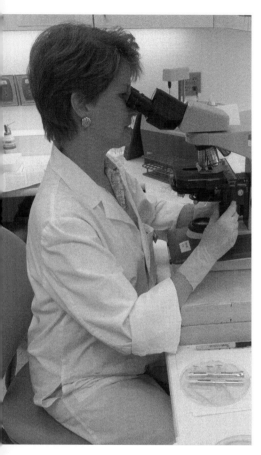

*Elizabeth Dole's trans-
formation of Red Cross
blood collection procedures
included regular testing for
diseases such as HIV or
hepatitis. Thanks to the
success of the program, the
nation's largest blood
supplier is also among
its safest.*

and of the blood supply. Mrs. Dole has been very tough-minded about raising the standards."

However, transformation didn't take place nearly as quickly as Red Cross critics would have liked, and it ended up costing $287 million, nearly three times as much as initially estimated. In 1993, the Food and Drug Administration became so upset with the slow pace of change in Red Cross operations—even as the AIDS crisis was mounting—that it obtained a court order forcing the agency to upgrade blood services according to a strict five-year plan.

Today, the Red Cross's blood services program receives passing grades from the FDA. But transformation cost the agency more than the millions of dollars it took to reorganize; there was also the cost in lost goodwill from the volunteers who had manned blood drives for decades, but who, unless they agreed to undergo extensive training, were now relegated to serving soft drinks and cookies.

In addition, volunteers and Red Cross staffers at several remote blood centers were annoyed that National Headquarters had exerted so much control over them. In fact, in 1995, employees and the board of directors at the Ozarks unit became so fed up with their diminished role that they broke ties with the Red Cross and formed their own blood bank.

It was about this time that Bob Dole's third presidential campaign went into full swing. Mrs. Dole raised eyebrows at blood centers for taking a leave of absence from her position to help her husband campaign just when emotions were running highest. "Frankly I was shocked that they would allow her to take a one-year leave of absence and then come back," the chairman of the Louisville, Kentucky, blood unit told *Time*. "That's pretty hard for an organization to deal with, while [its] president goes on hiatus to campaign for her husband."

What worried community blood banks that supply the nation's other half of blood, however, was the possibility Mrs. Dole would become first lady and still head the Red Cross—something she promised to do. "It's not reality. How could she come back?" a community blood center executive member said in an interview. "How could any action that she would ever make be viewed objectively?"

As fate would have it, Mrs. Dole didn't become first lady in 1996, and did return as head of the Red Cross. But by 1999, independent blood banks across the country were crying foul over what they perceived as another power play. Although transformation had been largely successful, it had strained Red Cross finances, creating a shortfall the giant nonprofit was trying to balance by collecting and selling even more blood than its competitors. Smaller nonprofit competitors complained that the Red Cross was using its clout to wrestle business away from other blood banks. (For example, agency officials asked the Defense Department to let the Red Cross be the sole recipient of military blood donations, a request that was denied.) Smaller businesses also accused the agency of selling blood so cheaply to hospitals that other companies couldn't compete.

In some parts of the country, the Red Cross's efforts have actually increased the numbers of people giving blood. Overall, however, fewer and fewer people nationally are taking the time to roll up their sleeves and donate at blood drives, a trend that is even more ominous to critics than competition between the Red Cross and other community blood banks.

*Bob and Elizabeth Dole wave to supporters at his birthday celebration in Russell, Kansas, on July 22, 1996. Bob Dole made his third bid for the presidency in 1996, and once again Elizabeth took a leave of absence from her job—this time as president of the American Red Cross—to help her husband campaign.*

# 9

# ON THE ROAD AGAIN

E lizabeth's work at the Red Cross on transformation and improving the agency's response to disasters was put on hold because of politics—her husband's, not hers. On April 10, 1995, Senator Bob Dole announced his third candidacy for president of the United States. In a far more unexpected move a year later, he publicly stepped down from his beloved Senate post to devote his full attention to the campaign and show the American public he had no safety net to fall back on. Afterwards, he said he had "nowhere to go but the White House or home."

He joined a field of Republican presidential candidates that would grow to include publisher Steve Forbes, Senator Phil Gramm, conservative commentator Pat Buchanan, former Tennessee governor Lamar Alexander, and Senator Dick Lugar.

By now well aware of the sacrifices a political spouse must make, Elizabeth relied on a time-tested technique and took a 14-month, unpaid leave of absence from the Red Cross. "What we women have worked for," she said, "is to be able to decide what's best for us and our families." However, one of her first promises on the campaign trail was to return to her post following the 1996 general election.

"There would be two President Doles if Bob is elected," Elizabeth said. "He will be President of the United States, and I'll be president of the Red Cross."

The press had a field day comparing Mrs. Dole and other candidates' spouses to First Lady Hillary Rodham Clinton, whom *Time* called Bill Clinton's "best asset and his worst liability." At the time, the *Congressional Quarterly Researcher* had this to say: "The travails of Hillary Rodham Clinton—criticism of her activism as well as questions about her credibility in the White water and "Travelgate" affairs—have reminded Americans that the proper role for a first lady remains an unsolved national puzzle."

Other observers agreed presidential wives were between a rock and a hard place, losers no matter how they acted as first lady. "Expectations for how a woman should speak are at odds with expectations for how a person with authority should speak," said Deborah Tannen, a Washington professor and writer. "If we speak as women are expected to, we aren't taken seriously, and if we speak with authority—as a lawyer is trained to speak—we're seen as not feminine and too aggressive. You can't win."

And by vowing to resume presiding over the Red Cross, Mrs. Dole invited criticism about how much power she would wield as head of a charity that, while not funded by the government, certainly deals with it. "If Hillary Clinton raises an eyebrow, the conflicts of Elizabeth Dole's running the Red Cross and living in the White House should levitate an entire body," Arthur Caplan, the director of the Center of Bioethics at the University of Pennsylvania, said in a 1996 *New York Times* article.

The election-year piece noted that Mrs. Dole had convinced the Bush Administration to permit the Red Cross to buy goods and services, such as cars and airline tickets, at the same discounts for volume buying that other government agencies—but not other nonprofits—receive. But despite the implications of Mrs. Dole's increased influence as first lady, Red Cross chairman Norman R. Augustine predicted government officials would make decisions on the merits, not perceived political pressures from her. "They know how to deal with those issues. You listen and then you do what you think is right."

Mrs. Dole's finances also underwent considerable scrutiny for the first time. Articles questioning management of a blind trust (personal investments made by a third party) and her failure to donate as much to the Red Cross as she had pledged hit the newsstands (she wrote a check for the remaining $75,000 she had promised to give, attributing the oversight to an accounting error).

But any weaknesses Mrs. Dole's campaign role revealed were usually far outweighed by the strengths she brought to the race. Her husband, after all, had dubbed her his "Southern strategy." Wherever she went preaching on Bob Dole's behalf, crowds reacted enthusiastically, especially at a visit to Salisbury for a ceremony intended to honor her. She nonetheless steered the spotlight toward her husband.

On that day, Mrs. Dole and the other speakers made a president's character the main topic of discussion. "This election, I believe, is about the character of our country as we move into the next century," said Elizabeth. "It is also about the character of the person who will lead us there. I commend you to a man of strong character: my husband, Bob Dole."

When it became apparent Bob Dole would win the Republican nomination and square off against Bill Clinton, the president suggested that the first lady and Mrs. Dole have their own public debate, surely an American first. (In his 1992 presidential campaign, Bill Clinton had suggested a vote for him was the equivalent of "buy one, get one free.") The University of Toledo took the lead and invited both women to debate "the role of the

Presidential spouse in American politics today," but Mrs. Dole declined without saying why and Mrs. Clinton's office didn't respond.

The media pitted the two women against each other nearly as much as the candidates. In one magazine spread, Mrs. Clinton was pictured touring a Czechoslovakian castle, just opposite a photo of Mrs. Dole in California with a familiar prop: a miniature rocking chair with sideways runners that she said belonged to President Clinton because "it rocked from left to right and back again."

The comparisons could be even more trivial, such as *Family Circle* magazine's bake-off issue, which made much ado of the wives' cookie recipes. Mrs. Clinton had inadvertently sparked the kitchen contest in the 1992 presidential contest with her famous "I suppose I could have stayed home and baked cookies" line. Nonetheless, her chocolate chip recipe was chosen by readers over First Lady Barbara Bush's recipe. This time around, Mrs. Dole, who had admitted being a stranger to the kitchen, sent in her mother's recipe for pecan roll cookies.

To boost their visibility with the American public, the Doles authorized a re-release of their 1988 autobiography, this time calling it *Unlimited Partners: Our American Story.* The updated version contained a few more details about Mrs. Dole's life, including her religious awakening, but concluded with a chapter that mostly laid out innumerable reasons why Bob Dole felt he would make a better president than Bill Clinton.

Although no one asked, conservative writer William F. Buckley Jr. announced his suggestion for Senator Dole's vice-presidential pick: Elizabeth Dole herself. She filled every possible qualification, he said: a Harvard lawyer; unparalleled experience in previous administrations; and, she was a woman. Mr. Buckley reasoned that because Bob Dole's campaign needed a spark of some sort, and his candidacy could use female support, Elizabeth was the perfect choice. The only problem, he

concluded, was the Secret Service rule prohibiting the president and vice president from flying together on Air Force One.

Easily the highlight of the campaign trail—at least for Mrs. Dole—was her smashing performance the night her husband officially received the nomination for president at the Republican National Convention in San Diego. There, she overshadowed every other speaker, including Pat Buchanan, Texas governor George W. Bush, and fiery House Speaker Newt Gingrich.

For the traveling media who had seen Mrs. Dole's talk-show host performances in action, her speech was nearly word-for-word the familiar "Why I love Bob Dole" pitch they had heard in small towns across America. But for millions of Americans to whom Elizabeth Hanford Dole was still something of a mystery, her folksy tribute to her spouse was a totally fresh and electrifying performance.

*Elizabeth Dole steps down from the convention stage, delivering an impassioned speech about her husband at the 1996 Republican National Convention. While the speech boosted Dole's campaign, it also made many members of the GOP consider Elizabeth as a possible candidate one day.*

*With running mate Jack Kemp, Bob Dole gives the thumbs up to reporters during his 1996 campaign. Unfortunately for the GOP, voters turned their thumbs down on the Dole-Kemp ticket, electing Democrat Bill Clinton to a second term with 49 percent of the vote.*

She began it by breaking tradition and walking from the podium down a long stairway to the center of the convention floor, telling the audience "it's just a lot more comfortable for me to [talk about my husband] down here with you."

"Bob Dole," she said, "if you're watching, let me just warn you, I may be saying some things that you in your modesty would never be willing to talk about." Moments later, giant television screens surrounding the podium where she began her remarks flashed the image of her husband sitting in his hotel room. Looking adoringly at him, she went on to list the reasons America should elect her husband: his humble beginnings in dirt-poor Russell, Kansas; the trauma and uphill recovery from his war injuries; his accomplishments in Congress; and his efforts on behalf of the disabled.

Mrs. Dole called the senator her own "personal Rock of Gibraltar," and noted for those who might mistake him for being sarcastic that he had twice been voted the friendliest of all 100 senators by Senate employees. Many of the audience members were awestruck by Mrs. Dole. "I think she walks on water," a San Diego businesswoman told the *New York Times*. "I think she'll make a phenomenal First Lady."

The morning after, the *Times* joined a chorus of profoundly impressed journalistic observers. "By all rights, today was Mr. Dole's day," the paper said. "But in truth his wife was the real center of attention, celebrated across this convention city for her politically deft and commanding performance as she wandered the audience for 20 minutes of seemingly scriptless conversation."

After the glow of the convention died down, Mrs. Dole continued her quest to boost her husband's appeal among female voters, a group strongly in the Clinton camp. She made upwards of 30 campaign appearances a week throughout the fall, delivering her 50-minute speech several times a day in different cities. Her pitch was universally warm and fuzzy: Bob Dole has helped disabled Americans by raising millions of dollars on their behalf, and he's also so trustworthy "you can take his word to the bank."

The only time she stepped out of her Southern belle character was when she appeared on *The Tonight Show* with host Jay Leno. Wearing black jeans, a leather biker's jacket and boots, she rode onstage on the back of Leno's Harley-Davidson motorcycle, saying "Rev it, baby. I've come a long way from Harvard Law School to biker chick." Why the uncharacteristic publicity stunt? "I had a chance to talk about my husband as a person," she explained afterwards in an interview. "People don't really know him as a person. And it was a fun thing to do."

In October, Mrs. Dole was a guest on *The Late Show with David Letterman*, where she ticked off the top-ten reasons to elect Bob Dole, including "Our dog, Leader, is much better at 'Stupid Pet Tricks' than Clinton's cat, Socks."

Meanwhile, her whirlwind campaign performances and television advertisements continued to generate enthusiastic responses and boost her opinion ratings in the polls. Were she running for president, political analysts agreed, women voters may have flocked to her camp. But Elizabeth's Herculean efforts were not translating into increased voter support on Bob Dole's behalf, and she constantly deflected questions asking whether she was courting the electorate for her own future benefit. She insisted she had "absolutely no plans" to seek office, which many political observers translated to mean, "but I'm also not ruling it out."

*Elizabeth Dole waves American flags during a March 1999 rally in her hometown. Supporters urged Dole to run for president in 2000, but as she always does Elizabeth carefully weighed all the pros and cons before making a decision.*

# 10

# DOLE 2000

Throughout Bob Dole's campaign, public opinion surveys indicated that half of all male voters supported him and about half were behind Bill Clinton. But try as he might to win over American women, the scales were tipped decidedly against him: 57 percent of women favored Clinton versus 43 percent for Dole. In the end, he would lose his third and final bid for the presidency to Bill Clinton in a race in which he could never seem to jump-start his candidacy.

Now retired from the Senate he knew so well, there was little left for him to do but fade from the political spotlight and pursue other opportunities, such as his appearance as a pitchman for VISA credit cards. Elizabeth, on the other hand, had the security of the Red Cross to fall back on, and in January 1997, she resumed the presidency she had vacated the previous year.

Despite her husband's defeat, she came away from the campaign a household name. A month after the election, *Glamour* named her one of its Women of the Year. Moreover, people couldn't help speculating that 2000 could be Bob Dole's turn to campaign for his wife. *Time* even cautioned readers not to get rid of those "Dole for President" campaign buttons just yet. Coy as always, Mrs. Dole opened the door just a crack, saying, "If at some point it seemed feasible, that there was an opportunity to run at whatever level, it is an option I might well consider."

In various interviews, she had already predicted a woman would be elected president—most likely by first becoming vice president—within her lifetime. What she failed to add was that she was without doubt among the most qualified women in the 20th century to do just that.

By 1998, two years before the next presidential election, familiar Republican names were already being bandied about: Bush, Quayle, Dole, and Kemp. But this time, it was George W. Bush, and not the former president, whose candidacy was considered likely. And this time, it was Elizabeth Dole, not Bob, who was mentioned as the darling of the GOP. The press noted that both were keeping high profiles thanks to their jobs—Bush as governor of Texas, Dole with the Red Cross—while talking quietly to fund-raisers.

Another possible candidate was House Speaker Newt Gingrich, a feisty conservative who was the GOP's greatest motivator at times and the party's worst nightmare at others. However, Gingrich's fate was sealed after the 1998 Congressional elections, when his leadership was blamed for the Republican Party losing several critical seats in the House and Senate. After taking stock of his wounded standing in the party, Gingrich announced he would resign as Speaker and step down from the House of Representatives, even though he had just been reelected.

Elizabeth Dole had no such political baggage to weigh her down. In fact, the attractiveness of her candidacy was becoming more and more apparent in 1998, as the country's attention was riveted on President Bill Clinton's relationship with Monica Lewinsky, a former White House intern.

Independent Counsel Kenneth Starr's investigation into questionable Clinton dealings like his Whitewater land investments had now zeroed in on the Lewinsky affair, which Clinton initially denied but later admitted to before a grand jury. Starr subsequently presented evidence to the House Judiciary Committee that he said proved the president had lied under oath and obstructed justice in the matter. For only the second time in history, the full House voted to impeach a president. However, with Republicans holding a majority of seats in the chamber, the vote was pretty much along party lines.

After a month-long trial in the Senate, where Republicans also had a majority, Clinton was acquitted of the charges, with neither count even getting a simple 51-vote majority, let alone the 67 needed to convict him.

However, the Lewinsky affair and the other scandals of the Clinton administration made Elizabeth Dole appear very attractive as a presidential contender, or at the very least the top vice presidential candidate. "She's never been so well positioned," one of her Red Cross advisers said in an interview. "She's an antidote to the problems of Clinton and the Democrats. All the events

*As the 2000 presidential race began heating up in the spring of 1999, Republican George W. Bush (center), the governor of Texas and son of Elizabeth's former boss President George Bush, was considered Dole's strongest competitor for the GOP nomination. Pundits speculated that whoever won the primary would face Vice President Al Gore in the general election.*

of the last six months have only helped her."

The publishers of *George* magazine certainly thought Mrs. Dole was a rising star. In September 1998, they named Elizabeth one of the 20 Most Fascinating Women in Politics. And for once, Bob Dole was singing her praises as speculation about her running for office grew. "Those of us who have stood in the political arena do not stand there alone," he said in the article. "Elizabeth has stood with me, cheerfully accepting the demands of politics, and I have rejoiced in her graces. And if she ever wants to enter the political arena on her own behalf, then I'm ready, willing, and able to stand with her."

But *Newsweek* noted that as a candidate, rather than the candidate's supportive spouse, Mrs. Dole would face a bruising campaign much different than she was used to. And if her goal was really to become the GOP's vice presidential candidate, she couldn't afford to "sit and wait for the phone to ring."

*Fortune* magazine ranked presidential hopefuls by odds: long shots, longer shots, and shots in the dark. Not surprisingly, Gov. George W. Bush topped the list, followed by "long shots" Steve Forbes and Senator John McCain. Elizabeth Dole, the only female mentioned, fell into the "longer shots" category along with Newt Gingrich, Jack Kemp, and Dan Quayle. The magazine called her the "best politician in the field, [even though] she's never run for public office." It added snidely, "But she was elected May Queen at Duke, which is one more beauty contest than most of these guys can claim."

Perhaps the most critical article written about Mrs. Dole's prospects in 1998 appeared in *National Review,* which recognized her popularity but questioned her substance. "She appeals to Christian conservatives and the party establishment, a rare combination," it said. "She can raise funds; everyone knows her name—her candidacy would have everything. Everything, that is,

but a rationale." Why? Because even though a successful politician, Mrs. Dole had managed to avoid
revealing just what her politics really were, or at least
how they had evolved.

Nevertheless, in December 1998, Republican
organizer Earl Cox took it upon himself to establish a
"Draft Elizabeth Dole" campaign, starting with opening a headquarters office in her hometown of Salisbury,
North Carolina. After that, he said he intended to
launch a similar push in Bob Dole's native Kansas.

Years before, Cox had tried to drum up support for
another "ideal" Republican candidate: retired General
Colin Powell, who became so famous for his role
in the Persian Gulf War that his name was constantly
mentioned as a presidential contender, despite
Powell's perennial protests that he was not interested
in running.

In a letter soliciting Republican support, Cox said
Elizabeth Dole "has an impeccable reputation for
being a person of high moral character. Her government and corporate experience have earned her a
reputation for being a strong and honest leader." He
added, "Untainted by politics, Elizabeth Dole is
well qualified."

Mrs. Dole couldn't seem to make up her mind. In
one speech, she ruled out running for office altogether.
But several months later, she again hedged her bets,
telling the *Salisbury Post,* "I have thought seriously
about it, and I've learned never to say never and then
sort of leave it there."

Finally, on January 5, 1999, Mrs. Dole took an irre-
versible step that made her intentions less murky. After
nearly eight years overseeing the Red Cross, she
announced her decision to resign within two weeks.
"At this important time in our national life, there may
be another way for me to serve our country," she said,
without spelling out how.

But in a subsequent interview, Mrs. Dole revealed

that she would make up her mind about whether to run for president in the days ahead. People close to her said the only thing that could prevent her from seeking the presidency was lack of political backing and financial support. Political insiders estimated a national campaign would cost a minimum of $25 million, a figure Gov. Bush was deemed capable of raising as well as Mrs. Dole, who had proven herself an energetic fund-raiser.

The Dole boosters set out to gauge whether their candidate had a high enough profile and could raise enough money to be a contender. In late January, they opened an office at the Watergate complex in Washington, D.C., and filled it with "unofficial" advisers that included several of Mrs. Dole's former staffers as well as political consultants.

Week by week Dole operatives hinted that their boss was close to an announcement. In early February, for example, one unidentified aide offered this familiar tease: "Yes, I think she will run, but she's the only one who knows for sure."

Her aides also indicated that Mrs. Dole would file papers with the Federal Election Commission in order to set up a presidential exploratory committee, which would allow her to officially begin fundraising.

The political courtship ritual continued on the eve of Mrs. Dole's speech before the Manchester, New Hampshire, Chamber of Commerce, which was honoring a local Citizen of the Year. But there was little doubt Mrs. Dole was using the event to test the election waters in this pivotal New England state. In 2000, it would be the site of the first presidential primary race. She stoked speculation further by saying the country needed a president "worthy of her people."

One political consultant to the GOP interviewed at the time agreed Mrs. Dole was a formidable candidate, but he wondered how she would fare in her first political venture. "She has an appealing personality, and she's already the most viable potential woman candidate to

ever consider running for president," Ed Gillespie said to a newspaper reporter. "The questions that I and others have, though, is what is her position on the issues. As that comes into focus, there are plenty of risks of turning off as many people as she attracts."

Lo and behold, a week later Mrs. Dole began tiptoeing into the issues before a thousand college and university administrators gathered in Washington, D.C. Her speech outlined an education program that revolved around teacher quality, school choice, and

*Like Elizabeth Dole, Hillary Clinton was also thinking about a high-profile election in the summer of 1999. The first lady was considering running for one of New York State's two U.S. Senate seats.*

education standards, themes already embraced by the Republican Party. She also promised to fight for additional federal funding for research.

Mrs. Dole certainly sounded like a candidate, reminding the audience that she was a former educator herself. "I've refused to join those who often find it expedient to turn teachers into rhetorical punching bags," she told the assembly. "Yes, we should expect the best out of our teachers. Yes, we should reward outstanding performances. But let us never forget that the true heroes of our society are not to be found on a movie screen or a football field. They are to be found in our classrooms."

In addition to all the anticipation surrounding Mrs. Dole's political plans, election year 2000 was shaping up to be the Year of the Woman in several other arenas. There was, for example, a deluge of media speculation over whether First Lady Hillary Rodham Clinton would decide to run in New York State for the U.S. Senate seat up for grabs following Daniel Patrick Moynihan's announced retirement.

The thought of a sitting first lady running for the Senate had initially seemed little more than a novelty, a trial balloon launched by a Democratic congressman. But after his remark struck a chord with journalists and New York Democrats, people were suddenly saying, "Yeah, why not?" Mrs. Clinton added fuel to the fire when she announced she would give "careful thought" to running, and then spent much of the summer of 1999 on a "listening tour" of the state.

However, political observers suggested that while a Hillary Rodham Clinton campaign would make an interesting sideshow, the main attraction would continue to be a woman running for president—or vice president. "It's not unlikely that both parties will put a woman on their presidential tickets, meaning that the United States would elect a woman as vice president for the first time," political consultant Jennifer Laszio was

quoted by Reuters. "I think it's going to happen."

Other political analysts agreed that a Dole candidacy would pressure the Democrats to at least come up with a female vice presidential candidate of their own, such as California senator Dianne Feinstein. "It is quite possible that both parties will nominate women for vice president and that would be very exciting," Ellen Malcolm, head of a political action committee that supported Democratic women, said in an interview.

There have been few women candidates for the nation's highest office. The first was Victoria Woodhull,

*Myrna Blyth, editor in chief of* Ladies' Home Journal, *presents the magazine's "One Smart Lady" award to Elizabeth Dole. No matter what happens in the 2000 presidential election, Dole will always be remembered as a Washington, D.C., groundbreaker and politician able to get things accomplished.*

who created the Equal Rights Party and ran as its presidential candidate in 1872. Woodhull, a controversial advocate of women's rights in a time when women were denied the right to vote, was in jail on election day, accused of sending obscene materials (pamphlets advocating women's freedom to divorce) through the mail. Belva Lockwood, a teacher and lawyer who was the first woman permitted to practice before the United States Supreme Court, supported Woodhull's 1872 campaign, and twice ran unsuccessfully for president herself, in 1884 and 1888.

In 1964, Senator Margaret Chase Smith, a Republican from Maine, became the first woman to seek the presidential nomination of a major political party. The first African-American woman elected to Congress, Shirley Chisholm of New York, campaigned for the Democratic presidential nomination in 1972.

While no woman has run in a presidential race since 1984, when Congresswoman Geraldine Ferraro of New York was Walter Mondale's running mate, female politicians have been making steady inroads into a profession that was once almost exclusively male. For instance, in 1986 Barbara Mikulski of Maryland became the first Democratic woman to win a Senate seat rather than be appointed to a vacant slot. After the 1992 election, the number of female senators increased from two to six, and the number of congresswomen rose from 29 to 48. By 1998, nine of the 100 Senate seats were held by women.

In hindsight, Geraldine Ferraro may not have been the right woman at the right time when she ran for vice president in 1984. In addition to media questions about her husband's financial dealings, the country simply appeared unready to put a woman in the White House just one step from the Oval Office. Indeed, 15 years later, Elizabeth Dole was the first one since then who was given half a chance of either becoming the first female president or, more likely, the first vice president.

As it turned out, of course, she was never able to generate the kind of enthusiastic support for her own candidacy that she seemed to spark whenever campaigning on her husband's behalf in previous presidential bids. There was considerably more press coverage of her before she began testing the presidential election waters than after she left the American Red Cross and began tiptoeing into them. In fact, her decision to withdraw from the race on October 20, 1999, barely generated ripples on the Election Year 2000 campaign trail, for by that point George W. Bush not only overshadowed his few remaining Republican opponents, but held a substantial lead in public opinion polls over Vice President Al Gore, who was himself struggling to win the Democratic Party's nomination.

Although Mrs. Dole backed out of the presidential race, no one knew for certain whether she might end up back on the Republican ticket as Bush's eventual vice-presidential running mate. Certainly, a female candidate would have obvious appeal to American women voters. Even Mrs. Dole once predicted a woman would be elected president of the United States—in her lifetime—most likely by first gaining office as vice president.

In any event, we probably haven't heard the last of Elizabeth Dole. The Duke May Queen, Harvard lawyer, cabinet secretary, and humanitarian executive has time and again shattered the proverbial glass ceiling during her enviable career, opening the way for other women to also make it to the top. She seems unlikely to "go gently into that good night" with so much accomplished, but something left to prove.

# CHRONOLOGY

1936    Mary Elizabeth Alexander Hanford born to John and Mary Cathey-Hanford in Salisbury, North Carolina

1954    Graduates from Boyden High School in Salisbury; enrolls as political science major at Duke University, North Carolina

1958    Graduates with Phi Beta Kappa honors from Duke University, and a B.A. in political science; moves to Boston, Massachusetts, and becomes secretary to the head librarian of Harvard Law School Library

1960    Earns a master's degree in education and government from Harvard

1962    Enrolls in Harvard Law School

1965    Graduates from law school and moves to Washington, D.C.; takes a job with the Department of Health, Education and Welfare

1968    Takes a job with the Johnson administration in the White House Office of Consumer Affairs

1970    Chosen Outstanding Woman of the Year in Washington, D.C.

1973    Nominated and confirmed by the Senate to a vacancy on the Federal Trade Commission

1975    Marries Kansas Senator Robert Dole in Washington, D.C.

1976    Takes leave of absence from the FTC to campaign for President Gerald Ford and her husband, who is named his vice presidential running mate

1979    Resigns from the FTC to go on the campaign trail for Bob Dole's first presidential bid

1981    Appointed director of President Ronald Reagan's White House Office of Public Liaison

1983    Joins Reagan's cabinet advisors as secretary of transportation

1987    Steps down as transportation secretary to campaign for Bob Dole's second presidential run

1989    Becomes the secretary of labor in President George Bush's cabinet

1990    Leaves the Bush cabinet to become president of the American Red Cross in early 1991

1991    Launches "transformation," the $287 million overhaul of the Red Cross's blood services program

1995    Takes a 14-month, unpaid leave of absence from the Red Cross to campaign for Bob Dole's third presidential bid

1997    Rejoins the Red Cross as president

1999    Announces her resignation from the Red Cross and subsequently forms an exploratory committee to raise funds for her own presidential challenge in 2000; withdraws from the presidential race in October.

# FURTHER READING

Dole, Bob, and Elizabeth Dole, with Richard Norton Smith and Kerry Tymchuk. *Unlimited Partners: Our American Story.* New York: Simon and Schuster, 1996.

Lucas, Eileen. *Elizabeth Dole: A Leader in Washington.* Brookfield, CT: The Millbrook Press, 1998.

Mulford, Carolyn. *Elizabeth Dole: Public Servant.* Hillside, NJ: Enslow Publishers, 1992.

Reitman, Judith. *Bad Blood: Crisis in the American Red Cross.* New York: Kensington Publishing, 1996.

Wertime, Marcia. *Bob Dole.* Philadelphia: Chelsea House Publishers, 1997.

White, Jane, and Elizabeth Dole. *A Few Good Women: Breaking the Barriers to Top Management.* Upper Saddle River, NJ: Prentice Hall, 1992.

# INDEX

# PICTURE CREDITS

page

| | | |
|---|---|---|
| 2: Courtesy of the American Red Cross | 39: Corbis/Bettmann-UPI | 72: Corbis/Bettman-UPI |
| 12: AP/Wide World Photos | 40: Corbis/Bettmann-UPI | 76: Corbis/Bettmann-UPI |
| 16: AP/Wide World Photos | 43: Corbis/Bettmann | 78: Reuters/Corbis-Bettmann |
| 18: Duke University Archives | 47(top): Corbis/Bob Rowan; Progressive Image | 81: Reuters/Corbis-Bettmann |
| 20: Corbis-Bettmann | 47(inset): Corbis/Bettmann-UPI | 84: Corbis/Owen Franken |
| 25: Duke University Archives | 48: AP/Wide World Photos | 86: AP/Wide World Photos |
| 26: Duke University Archives | 51: AP/Wide World Photos | 91: AP/Wide World Photos |
| 27: Duke University Archives | 55: Corbis/Bettmann-UPI | 92: AP/Wide World Photos |
| | 56: AP/Wide World Photos | 94: AP/Wide World Photos |
| 30: Corbis/Bettmann-UPI | 60: Corbis/Bettmann-UPI | 97: AP/Wide World Photos |
| 33: AP/Wide World Photos | 64: AP/Wide World Photos | 101: AP/Wide World Photos |
| 36: AP/Wide World Photos | 67: Corbis/Bettmann-UPI | 103: AP/Wide World Photos |
| | 70: UPI/Corbis-Bettmann | |

**Richard Kozar** is a writer living in Latrobe, Pennsylvania, with his wife, Heidi, and daughters, Caty and Macy. He has authored several Chelsea House books, including a biography of Hillary Rodham Clinton in the WOMEN OF ACHIEVEMENT series.

**Matina S. Horner** was president of Radcliffe College and associate professor of psychology and social relations at Harvard University. She is best known for her studies of women's motivation, achievement, and personality development. Dr. Horner has served on several national boards and advisory councils, including those of the National Science Foundation, Time Inc., and the Women's Research and Education Institute. She earned her B.A. from Bryn Mawr College and her Ph.D. from the University of Michigan, and holds honorary degrees from many colleges and universities, including Mount Holyoke, Smith, Tufts, and the University of Pennsylvania.